# BEYOND
## *the*
# ORPHANAG E

**...A Journey of Hope**

Deborah Dzifa. ..........

ISBN:978-9988-53-943-6

For further information or permission, contact:
Deborah Dzifah Tamakloe +233 (0) 242 125 415
tamakloe.deborah@yahoo.com

First Publish: November 2020
Content Editing and Proofreading
Melody S. Quaku +233 (0) 276 129 868

**Cover Design**

Kelvin Boison +233 (0) 242 045 272

**Layout Design & Printing**

Print Innovation
+233 (0) 267 771 670 / +233 (0) 572 007 000
www.print-innovation.com
www.innovationbooks.net

Author photograph by Joshua Duneebon
Cover photo by Hong Sukyouni

Photographs are courtesy of the author unless otherwise
stated

# DEDICATION

Dedicated to care leavers and everyone who
played a role in making my life colorful.

# ACKNOWLEDGMENTS

I am very fortunate to have such lovely, supportive people in my life. My deepest gratitude goes out to my parents for bringing me into the world, nurturing me, and at a point, leaving me to experience life in the orphanage and to go beyond it. The thought of them keeps me going.

My heartfelt gratitude also goes to my guardian angels: Reverend Dr. Victor Ofori Amoah, whose orphanage I grew up in; Mama Vicky Enchia, who sponsored my Senior High School education; and Prophet Bernard El Bernard Nelson Eshun who sponsored my university education.

To all my tutors and lecturers, especially Reverend Dr. Edward Ebo Onumah, Professor Daniel Bruce Sarpong, Mrs. Roseline Asantewaa, Dr. Vanessa Omaro, Mr. Frank Akutey, Mrs. Grace Adzawude, I say God richly bless you.

To my roommates and course mates at the university, and my fantastic team at Charis Touch Foundation and Camp Grace, I am indebted to you all.

To my pastors, especially Prophet Vincent Bannerman, Pastor Henry Doe, Prophet Foster Elorm Azumah, Prophet Samuel Odonkor, Pastor Abu-Ibrahim, and the entire pastoral team of Spiritlife Revival Ministries and choristers, I say God bless you. You are all amazing.

To say this book is "by Deborah Tamakloe Dzifah" overstates the case. Without the major contributions made by other people, this book would certainly not exist.

I am immensely grateful to my first editor, Yerebakia Choro, for his thoughtful and insightful comments. Editor and Proof Reader Melody S. Quaku smoothed the bumps significantly. Wilson Ayinbangya Amooro drew it together at the end.

My thanks to Dr. Kwabena Frimpong-

Manso. He pored over every page with the utmost scrutiny bringing on board suggestions that make the book more readable. A special word of thanks to Jeremiah Lartey-Brown, who patiently nursed this book along until it came to the place that it is now. As I struggled to get my thoughts in print, I pictured all the meticulous people who dedicated weeks and, in some cases, months to this effort: looking over my shoulder, holding me accountable, and challenging me to create a final manuscript that met standards, worthy of their labor and contribution. God bless every one of you.

For offering diverse forms of support to keep me going in the making of this book, I remain indebted to: Mr. George Appiah Kwaasi, Mrs. Mimi Elbernard Nelson Eshun, Mrs. Vera Bannerman, Pastor Emmanuel Sakyi, Daniel Fianko, Selina Atoklo, Etornam Abu-Ibrahim, Nana Efua Benyaw, Dr. Charity Osei Amponsah, Philomena Osei, Anderson Ahwireng, Auguster Asantewa Boateng, Anorbea Linda, Mabel Amoah, Sandra

Anyawoe, Monica Tawiah, Silvia Baatuahene, Naomi Barnes, Nancy Asamoah, Evelyn Ofosu Appiah, Aisha Ganiwu, Yalley Kingsley, Ephia Biney, Selina Atoklo, Adeta Samuel, Linda Kodua, Celestina Danso Arhin, Richard Larweh, Acheampong Samuel, Amanor Ruth, Vida Tetteh, Jude Kolog, Lydia Opoku Boakye, Billton Lartey, Deborah Nana Ama Abbey, Adedolapo Alabi, Addey Prince, Emmanuel Appiah Kubi, Dawutey Joana, Commey Rachael, Irene Tule, Abdul-Wassie Farouk, Michael Mayedeen, Joana Baidoo, Julius Aseye Nurnoo, Rockyln Awurabena Benissan, and all my brothers and sisters from BASCO; I love every one of you.

My siblings, Grace Tamakloe, Dora Tamakloe, Daniel Akpalu, Martha Doku, and all my amazing family and friends, God bless every one of you. I wish I had enough space to give special mention to all the notable people whose paths have crossed with mine. I could not have survived beyond the orphanage alone without your diverse inputs. To those who did not find their names here, I sincerely apologize. They may not be on these pages, but I honestly carry them deep within me wherever I go.

Peace and love to all orphans and vulnerable children in the various care homes. It is my hope that this book will inspire and teach you that there is no mountain too high to climb. And now to the amazing care leaver out there; I am so proud of your willpower, strength, and ability to get to wherever you have gotten to now in life. Thank you for not giving up but pressing on regardless of every storm. Do you have unfulfilled dreams? Well, I am sorry you could not fulfill some of your dreams as you wish. But always know that it is never too late to chase those dreams again. I love you for not losing hope. I love you for being relentless. Always walk with your head up, knowing that numerous people in the world pray for you and wish you well.

Love,
Deborah Dzifah Tamakloe.

x

# Notes

- **Care leaver:** An adult who has spent some time in a foster or residential care and has left to live on their own.

- **Our father**: Founder of the Baptist School Complex and Orphanage (BASCO).

- **The Home:** Baptist School Complex and Orphanage (BASCO)

- **Care Home**: Orphanage or residential care facility

- **Siblings**: Other children in the Care Home

# CONTENTS

# FOREWORD

This book creates awareness of care leavers in Ghana, that is, young people who have left care homes to live on their own. For too long, our focus has only been on supporting children in residential homes and not entirely on care leavers. In this book, the author brings to light the grim truth that without society's support, the future of care leavers' is unpleasant.

The *let-it-all-hang-out* honesty made her writing not only accessible but relatable, for beneath all the scenes and fantastic stories were recognizable human characters and emotions. This book is highly original. I think it makes the weather on so many vital topics, such as the real scuffles of care leavers.

While it may make some people (including experts and the media) uncomfortable, we need not just read, but listen as well. The book blends timeless and relevant knowledge, in the here and now, and ahead of its time.

Through honest communication and tenacious playfulness, Deborah boldly and bravely seeks, through her writing, to be the voice of the numerous care leavers in the world.

I am privileged to write the foreword for Deborah, a close friend, and someone who inspires me to work harder.

Dr. Kwabena Frimpong-Manso

(Senior Lecturer, University of Ghana)

# PREFACE

If you ask me what the best interests of care leavers are, I will answer by saying: "pay close attention to them, because they need more than food, clothes, and a roof over their heads. They need role models and helpers."

You may be holding this book for a couple of reasons: probably because you want to satisfy your curiosity about care leavers or because you love care leavers and want to identify with their needs and wants. For whichever reason you are holding this book, I need you to know you have made the right choice. I need you also to know that it does not cost much to change a care leaver's life. Yet, to them, your decision can mean the difference between life and death.

No one knows how hard it was for me to write this book. For some reason, I found it more difficult writing than sharing the story orally. I did not want to write an inspirational book. I wanted to give people something real and hard-hitting to help them appreciate the 'life beyond the orphanage'.

I stopped writing many times because I had to retreat to let go of the humiliations and pains and release forgiveness to people who caused me great hurt. I agonized over relieving my heart of the pains of those experiences, and I wept for joy that I did it. While some of the memories brought a renewed sense of happiness, some brought depths of tears to the surface, and yet others brought to mind precious moments long forgotten.

As you read this book, I invite you to pray with me and all care leavers. I still recall most of my mates' plans, dreams, and aspirations back in the Home. Great ideas they were, but not many of those ideas found realization.

I have come across adults who can't let go of the fond memories of their deceased parent(s.) They get heartbroken, and some get affected the whole time. Even in the state of their naivety, the younger ones (0-17 years) equally go through this same ordeal. They have to battle with the fact that their parent(s) are no more. They have to develop tough skins as they come of age. They have to fight even more challenging mêlées when they land in the orphanage; forging their ways through until they leave the care home. What next after they leave the Home? They then have to hustle their way through life, and if God doesn't intervene by sending helpers their way, the outcome is usually not pleasant. Many talents go wasted, and dreams are aborted. It will take you and me to be the voice of these vulnerable ones and raise awareness, so people start to look in their direction.

What is the use if we only donate to these youngsters whiles they are still at the orphanages or foster homes but can't support them when they leave the four walls of the care facilities? I have had interactions with many of my orphanage siblings and trust me; they have dreams like every other person. Like Martin Luther King Jr. (an American Christian minister and Social Activist) they have very great dreams, but the support system isn't there. The support structures in existence end the day they leave the orphanage.

I received a call recently from one of my orphanage sisters, who was lamenting on the phone that she was hungry. The first question I asked was: "are you not in BASCO?" (BASCO being the Home we both grew up). Her response was "no." Apparently, some workers from the Department of Social Welfare (DSW) came for her after she had completed Junior High School (JHS) and took her to a relative. Guess who the relative was: her sickly grandma! The unfortunate thing was that her grandma was also dependent on someone for a living, so until this beneficiary brought her grandma some food, she had to starve.

I received another call from one of my orphanage brothers one early morning on my way to work. After exchanging pleasantries over the phone, he expressed how grateful he was to God for my life. I asked him in which part of Ghana he was. In fact, his response broke my heart. Unknown to me, after he left the Home, he couldn't continue his education to the Senior High School (SHS) and had to resort to menial jobs for a living. Like the speed of light, my mind raced back to the visions we all shared back at the Home while growing up. What happened? I guess they never got a helper as I did.

Over the years, I realized that some codes are unwritten but have the most significant impact on our individual lives. Nobody teaches you these codes. You have to discover them yourself. Strangely enough, these codes are not taught in schools. Neither are they preached in any religious sanctuary. They, more often than not, come by experience, which may not be very amusing. If you happen to learn some of these unwritten codes, do well to share with others. I decided to share mine with you in this book.

I am not an overly adventurous young lady. My inkling of a daring journey is lying on the beach with my husband, a dense novel in hand while protecting my children from the scorching heat of the sun.

Like every human, I had ambitions too. The goal was to become somebody of high standing in the future. I didn't know how these ambitions were going to be achieved, but I kept hearing that education is the key to success, so I purposed in my heart to go to school no matter what. Most times, the dream is easily fulfilled when you have guaranteed support. In my case, I had a dream alright but did not know where the support was going to come from for the fulfillment of that dream. I had a desire to become a medical doctor. However, that dream changed the day I was admitted to the Agricultural Science class. I tried everything humanly possible to go to the Science class, but I was not allowed. Maybe I did not have anyone to hold my hand to the administration to plead my cause. Perhaps it was divine, and perhaps it was not. Whichever way, I am grateful to God for where I am now.

In spite of the giant leap I had ahead of me after I left the four walls of the orphanage, one thing kept me going, and that is the power of prayer, which I was taught at the residential home. I knew with prayer; there will always be a support. I have come to realize that I discovered myself in my struggles, and this discovery has increased my desire to live. I have been in some of the world's horrible situations, and I have learned from people who had turned pain into wisdom and suffering into strength.

The idea of this book, *BEYOND THE ORPHANAGE*, came to me one day as I went with friends to donate to an orphanage.

Like every other time, I always would like to observe and watch my friends do all the talking and handing over of items. As I looked at the children giggling and smiling, I recalled with a beaming chortle my childhood days in the children's home, the people I grew up with, the good times we had, and while I reminisced, I began to think aloud if these memories of how far I had come should stay with me or I should share them with the hope of paving the way for these innocent young-looking individuals. I came back to my room that day with so much in mind.

As I laid flat on my back with my face staring at the ceiling, I remembered a sermon my pastor preached in church. He mentioned that it is always great to turn one's pain into something positive. In other words, whatever you have survived should not be kept only to yourself, but rather be shared to inspire others. I sprang off the bed and grabbed my notepad, and that is how this book was birthed.

The book thus aims to tell the story of my life in and after I left the orphanage and give some practical recommendations for all stakeholders to make informed decisions to devise realistic and sustainable exit strategies for care leavers. I hope my story will inspire people to reach out to children in orphanages and those who have left these care facilities and those on the streets to help them create the world they always imagined living in.

Although my experience may not be the same as other care leavers from other orphanages or foster homes, I hope it paints a vivid picture of life in and beyond the orphanage.

Come with me as I take you briefly to my life in the orphanage and, most importantly, how I have survived as a care leaver.

## Chapter 1

## INTRODUCTION

## BEFORE THE ORPHANAGE

*March 1993*

It was a cold and quiet Monday night in a remote town called Nkawkaw, somewhere in the Eastern part of Ghana. As the clock struck midnight, making way into a new day, the cry of a baby was heard in simultaneous rhythm with the ticking of the clock announcing its arrival into the world. "This one is destined to be a strange child," the medical attendant tending to the new mum told her, considering the series of surgeries she was put through before she had the child. That new mum was my mum, and the 'strange' child, I. Am I a strange child? Well, I leave that for time to tell.

My family was a polygamous one: dad had four wives including my mum. That meant I had three additional mothers. We lived in Nkawkaw, where dad worked as a commercial driver and a farmer until he relocated with my mum to the village where his farms were located so he could properly monitor them. My dad had a model kind of body: thick tall with a beardless face and a dark shiny skin. As far as I knew, he was every woman's dream. As a commercial driver, passengers always called him by the famous inscription on his vehicle; "Sow in tears and reap in joy." I heard him chant this quote on several occasions with the town folks. But for his excessive love for women which served as a dent on his persona, he was highly respected in the community.

On a regular day, I always woke up every morning to his loud rosary recitations, and though I will usually bury my head back into my cover cloth to catch some more sleep, his loud whistling as he washed his car made sleep elude me even the more until I was completely knocked off bed. I would storm off to check the time in the living room; time check was usually around 4:30am, and the day had begun for me. Though I was usually agitated by this, I had no choice than to grab a lantern and begin to sweep in and around the house.

Sweeping was much easier because it produced less dust due to the stones and gravels in the house. That saved me from inhaling dust. During the dry season, when the amount of dust increased, before I swept, I would sprinkle some water on the ground to reduce the potential quantum of dust that will be generated.

As usual, my mum would be fast asleep, and I always wondered if she had some noise resisting buds in her ears. She had little formal education and did not have much those days as far as wealth is concerned. Yet, she is one of the wisest, truly generous women I have ever known. She was that woman that everyone turned to when in need. She was a beautiful piece, with beautiful light skin, charming looks with a very long and curly hair. I am always tempted to believe she won my dad's heart with her skin and charming looks. She was the "let go" type of person, easily forgiving people who offend her, most especially my dad. On days she is despondent, she could be heard singing all gospel hymns and would eventually switch to singing sorrowful songs. All those songs, as far as I remember, were about life and the afterlife.

I suppose I was indeed a strange child as I was struck by all strange manner of ailments ranging from bleeding nose, headaches, measles, fever, etc. now and then. Most notable among them was when my head began to grow unusually big. This condition was not so common. In a bid to find a remedy for my condition, which kept worsening every passing day, I was shuffled from one medical center to another, made to sniff some drugs including local herbs among others. That was not a pleasant experience for a young growing child! At a point, the growth reduced a bit but was still very much visible, turning me into an object of laughter and mockery for my school mates and other children in the community. I heard derogatory comments like "As for Dzifah, we can hide behind her occiput for shelter when it rains" "Hey, Dzifah, don't ever try to look up at a plane in the skies, else your head is gonna fall." How possible? Such mean comments!

The village I grew up in Ehiawoanwu was not a big one. Farming was the main economic activity for the village folks. Crops produced included both cash and staple crops. On a regular day, the singing of birds, the cocks' crows, the singing of drunkards and honking of cars, ushered in a new day. It was much fun in those days. Little children went to the community tap side in just their panties and sometimes even naked to fetch water. There was much serenity and safety with no worry over a child being sexually abused. Hardly would one hear of the mysterious death or disappearance of children. Not so much of that can be said in our today's world, you know!

The village had one video center where all manner of movies was shown for all. It was an exciting opportunity for us to watch TV since we never had the privilege of owning one in our homes. On such days when exciting shows are going on, I always dreaded mum coming with a long cane to drive us away from the video center whenever we had stayed out for too long or late into the night. And she always showed up without fail! Life was fun back then. We were only two girls at that time until my kid sister landed, and we became three in number.

One of my biggest fear had always been of the night, as I used to have recurring nightmares about dragons. I hardly knew what a good sleep was as I would regularly toss and turn for hours during the night because of horrible nightmares. It was so bad that I always woke up at midnight, screaming for my mum. I did not know the name 'Jesus' so well, though I was born into a Catholic family and was a Bible reader in my local church.

Being raised by both parents during my early childhood days was superb, but short-lived… It ended abruptly when I returned from school one day to meet my mum crying. Something unusual might have happened. Though she never opened up to me on what had happened, I had a strong suspicion my dad had a hand in it.

Shortly after this incident, my mum sent me to live with her friend in the nearby town to get to school on time. My school was several miles away from where we lived. Though my dad was a driver, I never got the privilege of riding in his vehicle to school. Either his vehicle was always full of passengers, or he left home late. Back then, any pupil who reported to school after 7am was punished. It was mostly corporal punishment such as canning. Thus, to avoid being punished in school for lateness, I would usually join some friends very early to walk several miles to school. These were the reasons mum gave to support her decision to send me to live with someone else in the next community. All the same I knew there was a deep reason. Yet, I was not in any position to find out.

As mum and I journeyed to my new abode, my mind was lost in time, drifting from the present as I reflected on the stories I had heard on how children who lived with others other than their parents were mistreated.

My memories took me to a storybook I read entitled *The Wicked Stepmother*. As I slowly recounted that book's events, I got scared and cried within because I thought I was going to be subjected to the same ill-treatment that was meted out to the victim in that story. Mum realized I was in thoughts…she would turn to look at me intermittently, but I always took my eyes off to gaze at the colorful birds and trees by the roadside. At that instance, when I saw a bluebird, I wished I could turn into one too and fly away to a distant place where I would not be seen: children and their weird thoughts.

We finally arrived in the town of Akoase. I dragged one bag as my mum carried my other bag to my new residence. We were met with a smile from my new guardian, and as she continued to smile at me, the wicked stepmother picture I had painted in my head diminished. She was slim in stature and married with five grown-up kids. On the other hand, her husband was directly opposite in terms of stature as he was huge and well built. After my mum left that evening, she gave me food and a place to sleep.

My new guardian was a petty trader, and her husband, a farmer. I was housed in the same room with their children. All their children were in the school-going age and were ahead of me except their last born. My stay with her was great as she gave me the best kind of treatment. Indeed, some people are kind. Mostly during weekends and vacations, I would go to my mum and return when school re-opens.

Everything was just perfect until after a year when my aunt came visiting my mum one weekend. As I eavesdropped on their conversation, I got to know my mum has decided to take me to a boarding school. I overheard them talking about this boarding school with much passion and decided to listen even more attentively. I heard my aunt telling my mum that the school was good and would help me become more stable and reduce my movement from one place to the other. She also added that due to the troubles in their marriage and her health status (my mum was then suffering from serious arthritis), sending me to that school would keep me focused on my studies.

I was so much excited about the school in question already and wished we went that same day. As I continued to listen, my mum sent me to buy tomatoes from our neighbor's shop. I got pissed as that meant I would miss a lot of the conversation about the school in question by the time I returned. I did not have a choice than to attend to Mum's call anyway. I dragged my feet to pick up the money from her until my aunt screamed. Her screaming sent me running out of the house, and by the time I returned, the conversation had ended, and my case was concluded: I was to be taken to a boarding school.

## *Chapter 2*

## WHERE IT ALL BEGAN

*January 2005*

**In the Beginning…**

It is not a beautiful experience to be separated from one's parents, especially if you are being taken to a place that does not have all the niceties your Home had. That fateful day was a regular Saturday morning in our home village. But it wasn't regular for me. It was the day I had to be chillingly separated from my Home and taken to a place I never dreamt I would find myself.

Prior to this, my mum decided to send me to a boarding school to help me become stable and focus well on my studies. Thus, after all the necessary preparation, mum and I set off to the much talked about boarding school to help me stabilize and focus on my studies.

Dad wasn't home when we left, but I wasn't bothered because I knew he was aware.

We spent the night at my aunt's house in Suhum; because the night caught up with us, and we could not continue to the school. I was excited because I thought the school was in Suhum since, as compared to where I was coming from, it was a city. Suhum is the capital of the district, i.e., the Suhum/Kraboa/Coaltar district. "I am finally moving from the village to the city," I thought to myself... However, that fantasy vanished into thin air when my mum said we had to travel the next day to the school.

We continued our journey the next day. We journeyed beyond cities and towns and entered a deep village. The road seemed unending as every new bend revealed a different aspect of the road. My heart began to skip very fast as the journey looked more like going into a thick forest than a school. I was lost and felt like Alice in wonderland. I imagined the journey as the hole Alice mistakenly entered.

"What good thing could come out of a school in such a location?" I asked myself. As I began to reflect harder, there was this sharp bend ahead, and just after the bend was the school "BAPTIST SCHOOL COMPLEX AND ORPHANAGE. "Is this supposed to be my new school and Home? But why would I be brought to an orphanage when both of my parents were still alive?" I had asked myself several questions.

The feelings were extremely challenging to comprehend; given that I was only 11 years at the time. Adjusting to the new environment didn't come on a silver platter as it took me time to appreciate the situation that Baptist School Complex and Orphanage (BASCO) was my new Home. A home I had to become acquainted with, and learn to adapt to. I had to accept, and comply with the new rules of my new home. If I wanted to survive, I had to learn all the survival tactics. In the mind of an eleven-year-old girl at the time, it was something too much to ask for.

The journey ahead sure did appear long and hard to believe at the time. Growing up, all I wanted was to grow into a beautiful woman, marry a handsome husband, and have a beautiful family. To find myself mingling with orphans and vulnerable children while having both parents alive wasn't a piece of easy ice to break. Neither was it a pleasant experience to be pushed at an early age into the drab uncertainty of orphanage routine. Yet, I survived. In fact, I did not merely survive, I triumphed!

We lived in the orphanage as siblings, developing a sense of togetherness and ethics of conduct characterized as codes. Honesty was a trademark of our words and actions, as we learned that our words reflected who we were and could not be taken back once spoken. We also established codes of conduct for ethical behavior that shaped our sense of morality and would stay with us throughout our lives. We made friends with some staff members who were very much likable, while some other staff members represented "government" and chastisement. No student dared misbehave in their presence. At the same time, and this should not come as an amazement, we did not share our innermost feelings or our remembrances of past sufferings.

Sharing of feelings was not done by most of us. We revealed surfaces to each other but we generally did not introspect; there may have been too much scar tissue for this, and also many of us probably could not deal with the inner pain of others.

Although I have not forgotten the ache of loneliness, which we could not understand, but could feel only too well, what remains in my brain case is the better moments, the common beliefs that we shared, the sense of affinity and friendship, and the feeling that we were somehow different from everyone else. The Home was many things to all of us at different stages of our lives there, but throughout, it remained our community; a self-contained, yet diverse conglomeration of boys and girls, adult supervisors, other caretakers, plus thieves, and bullies.

And yet, when I think of The Home, it is with very strong feelings of affection and gratitude. Simply stated, it is where I have lived. For good or ill, it is my point of reference. It was my home.

We formed study groups among ourselves and created an acronym to keep us going. It was DBAT (Determination Brings about Transformation), which we chanted anytime we saw ourselves at the Home. I was not sure what success meant, but it was a phantom I chased with unwavering determination. Today, although I may carry scars, they are healed lacerations—signifying life's struggles and the aspirations of a determined young lady. I can now work and love, and while I live very much in the present, I can talk for hours about the past.

I recall we had no electricity at the orphanage. We used a generator that gave light two hours daily from 7pm to 9pm. Most of those times were what we called prep hours i.e., after school studies. The switching on of the generator was always accompanied by bells' ringing to summon us to our respective classes for studies. Since the generator was only on for at most two hours daily, most of the final year students who usually studied extra hours at dawn did so with candles.

The Home produced their first batch of graduates (JHS graduates) in 2005. I was part of the third batch of final year students to complete JHS in 2007. My batch was made up of seven male and five female candidates. As usual, I was the smallest. Though I excelled in the class since I entered the orphanage, I was a bit anxious about what grades I would get in my final exams and whether those grades would get me admission into a good SHS. I had serious ambitions to make 'ten ones,' that is, get grade one in all ten subjects. *(NB: Grade one means excellent or distinction on the grading scale).*

As far back as I can remember, I was the first person to wake up every dawn among my year group. We were awoken from our sleep by the constant crow of the cock, shortly accompanied by the early morning rising bells. As soon as we heard the rising bell, we (final year students) would carry our books to the class with our lighted candles while the juniors went about cleaning the compound. Going to the classroom to study at dawn didn't continue for long as the morning air always blew off our candles. We devised another strategy: to spread our mattresses on the dormitory's corridor to study. That way, we had our candles all lighted and glowing like the early morning sun.

Hours turned to days, and days turned to weeks, weeks turned to months, and all too soon, it was time for the final exams at the JHS level, which is the Basic Education Certificate Examination (BECE). Our examination center was in the next town, so we had to commute daily for the five days that the exams lasted. The school's driver picked us up at 7am every morning. While on the bus, one could sense the exams tension in the air as book pages flipped. I got encouraged the more as I saw my mates all serious with their heads buried in their notebooks. Random questions were thrown at each other in the bus, and anybody with the answer could attempt it. The orphanage brought us food at the center daily. Fortunately for us, we got one mission house where our past questions and notes were kept, and that was where we had our breakfast and lunch as well. Everything progressed successfully until we were done writing the exams, and it was full of mixed feelings.

On the last day of the exams, a new 'us' emerged as the bus was filled with roars of victory songs. We sang and danced our hearts out. It was as if our driver understood our mood... he increased the bus's speed to suit the occasion. As we approached the school, the driver kept honking, signifying our victory. Our younger siblings were also ready with white powders at the school's gate to sprinkle on us. We all looked like we're going for a Halloween night as the powders poured on us turned us into different figures. After jubilating for over an hour, we gathered and prayed about the exams, asking God to help us come out with flying colors. We all departed into our various dormitories.

Something interesting happened that evening at the Home. That night, most of us didn't have our evening bath as we were dead tired and stressed out. One of our mates (a guy) nearly scared the hell out of a little boy with his white powdered face. The little boy thought he had seen a monster when he came outside to urinate.

## A short visit to my parents

*May 2007*

After completing our exams, some of my peers went to their relatives, and I also went to my parents. However, I found it rather difficult sharing the same space with my parents because their daily quarrels made it difficult for me to have my peace of mind. This situation aggravated and became too frequent that I broke down anytime they had a little misunderstanding. I never saw my parents play, laughing together, or hold a peaceful discussion; talk less of demonstrating some romance. The disunity was so conspicuous that as little as I was, I could clearly tell of the crack in our home, yet I could do nothing to bring them together. At the time of my visit, my parents had just rejuvenated their marriage vows and tied if off with a church wedding, but that didn't reflect one bit in their lifestyle. The problems kept worsening, and I knew the future wasn't going to be rosy for me. I could smell danger anytime they quarreled.

Preparations towards my going to senior high school did not tickle my dad. This nonchalance attitude of his was not novel anyway. It has always been that way since I went to the orphanage, and I don't blame him much. Who knows? Maybe shirking his responsibilities made me see life from a different perspective.

On the other hand, my mum managed to get me some provisions and a few other items I needed at the time. So, I only got an old trunk and returned to the orphanage when it was still left with two months for our BECE results to be released. I couldn't just wait to get back to the orphanage. I was even happy I was leaving my parents' because I found more comfort at the orphanage than in my own Home. What an irony!

Some few months after I had left my parents for the Home, news got to me that they had gotten divorced. My mum relayed the information to me, and for reasons known only to my dad, he shirked his responsibilities completely.

## Back to the Orphanage

The Home I grew up in wasn't the regular kind of orphanage. We didn't have it all, but we had God, and we had a good father and caretakers, which mattered a lot to us.

My hopes were high as I awaited my BECE. results, but you know, I was a bit anxious as well. Then one afternoon, the long-awaited news came: the results were out! One of our housemasters at the Home broke the news: I had made aggregate 11 and gained admission to Ghana Senior High School (GHANASS). My heart skipped a bit because the news he delivered wasn't what I was expecting to hear.

To him, I had done well, but I was disappointed. In the first place, I could not make my dream *10 ones*.

On top of that, I did not get my preferred choice of school—I wanted to go to a single sexed school, and GHANASS, which happens to be a mixed sexed school, was my third choice. At that moment, I felt like bursting out in tears or hitting the wall with my tiny fist and breaking it off or storming into the room and banging the door so hard. As all these thoughts were running through my mind, the housemaster stood smiling at me, and not knowing what was going on in my mind, he extended a hand to give me a congratulatory shake. As I was about to extend my hand to receive the handshake, he received a phone call and so I took advantage of the situation to run straight to my room and buried my face in my bed and sobbed to sleep.

The next big deal was to get a sponsor as school was to begin the following month.

On very few occasions, we had people coming to the orphanage to sponsor some junior high school graduates to further their education to the senior high school (SHS). But this wasn't common at all. Most of the very few sponsors were foreigners. I couldn't get any help from Home, and I wasn't expecting any as that was the gateway to disappointment. You see, as I mentioned earlier, I come from a polygamous family with more than 13 siblings. The home support was nothing to write home about except for my mum's support in providing the little she could.

Soon, senior high schools resumed for their first term, and first-year students were expected to report to school. I couldn't go because I had not gotten a sponsor. About two of my peers in my year group at the orphanage got sponsors and went to SHS. That was another hard time for me: watching the people I did better than go to school while I idled around wasn't comfortable. I began to ask myself many questions as fear gripped me. I always imagined myself wearing my SHS uniform and cat walking. And oh, I dreamt about it countless times. Most times in the afternoons, my pleasant dreams were always cut short by students wanting me to be the judge over their quarrels or some others who came checking up on me. I always gave such students a heavy blow on their faces in my head and eyed them hard for interrupting my nice dream. This show of displeasure for their interruption only happened in my head. They never materialized.

All too soon, the first term ended, and I still had no benefactor. I prayed all manner of prayers and believed God to show up for me, but I got no answer until the second term. I had a habit of crying my heart out to God anytime I prayed. On one occasion, while praying in the school's piggery, a tailless lizard wriggling itself nearby caught my attention. It looked like it wasn't bothered about the nonexistence of its tail. As I watched it run into the bush, I realized that we don't only need to wait for everything to be perfect before we get excited about life. Sometimes, we have to look beyond our challenges and embrace life with much positivity. I consoled myself and prayed without shedding any more tears that afternoon. I finished praying and felt very good within. I knew God made that lizard come around, so I see things from a different angle.

But you know it is always hard-hitting when you see people you believed God together with for the same miracle get theirs without struggle, whiles yours seem delayed. When this happens, people are tempted to think probably, you are not serving God well, or are living in sin, or most likely, your' house witches' are haunting you. It is intriguing how people sometimes think or quickly judge and associate one's situation to an unfortunate fate in life. They tend to forget that our God is a God of times and seasons and a prayer-answering one too. And when the time comes for each person to receive their blessings, nothing hinders them.

Despite my constant prayers without the immediate response as expected, I never felt betrayed. I knew by hook or crook; my ultimate helper remains the living God. I, therefore, put myself together and waited patiently for my season to unfold.

## Concluding comments

In my opinion, most children taken to orphanages suffered a grievous shock by merely being eligible for admittance to a residential home. Too many of us are admitted without any emotional preparation or without being accompanied by an understanding guardian or a loving family member. Although there are several reasons why a child is admitted into an orphanage with some of the reasons being abandonment, death of a parent, physical or mental challenge of the parent(s), poverty, conflict situations, or imprisonment of parents, it is recommended that before relatives or a parent(s) take their child to an orphanage; the child should be well informed of why they are being taken there, the harsh realities among others even if at that time their mind cannot process the information.

Such preconditioning will ensure that care leavers do not become bitter towards their relatives after they leave the various care homes. In my case, for instance, I only reconciled with my dad in 2016. Before that, I always saw him to be a wicked Dad. I had to consciously forgive him and check up on him from time to time after I had convinced myself enough that everything happens for a reason. But other care leavers might not be able to forgive their parents or relatives as I did.

Also, caretakers in residential homes should love every child placed in their care to ease the burden in these children's hearts.

# *Chapter 3*

## THE WAITING PERIOD

*August 2007*

### Becoming a teacher

As I waited for my time to go to the SHS, I decided to help teach the Kindergarten (KG) class at the Home. The Home did not have a teacher for that class, so I chose to teach them to keep myself busy while trusting God for a breakthrough to enter into the SHS.

These children always have a way of brightening my day. During forty winks hours in class, I got motivated as I watched them sleep off without struggle. No wonder God's requirement for inheriting His Kingdom is for one to be like a child. They have a free spirit. They were oblivious to my troubles. They kept mentioning my name every second as either one wants to use the washroom or report the case of a bully. Sometimes, I felt like they were too troublesome, but they proved very lovely, even in their troublesome state.

I always took them to the library in the afternoons and helped them read books such as novels and poetry. I helped them out with mathematics too. During this same period, I also got the opportunity to read some books at the library. I learned new vocabularies, and in a way, those books helped me relieve the burden in my heart. You know books have a way of blurring the burdens in one's spirit? They sometimes minister to you as a song does.

On few occasions, when my hurt was overly heavy, I would drift into sleep in the library and usually woke up to scattered books all over the library. These children were indeed at it again.; as I arranged each book back onto their respective shelves, I blamed myself for sleeping that deep. Staying awake would have reduced the mess these children always created.

I always wished I could lay hands on one of these children, and I would make him or her pack every book, but alas, the school would have closed already.

As the months progressed, my other siblings returned from their various SHS's for vacation and shared their first term's experience with the little ones and me. Although I was happy for them, I wished I could have a similar story to share. You will bear with me that someone's story is never yours, no matter how inspiring it can be.

The second term came, and just like the previous term, I watched my siblings pack their luggage and left for school, leaving me behind again. Well, I went back to the KG class with an aching heart to teach, just like I did beforehand. At least they kept me busy: an opportunity for me not to worry a lot.

**My time finally came**

My prayers, thankfully, did not go down the drain. A month after the second term had begun, our father came to the Home one day and told me to pack my luggage and leave for school immediately. My heart leaped for joy, but it was short-lived as I began to wonder how I could leave for school immediately since I didn't have any more provisions remaining except my soaps, a little gari (*a crisp and crunchy West African food made from grated cassava with the excess liquid dried out)*, and sugar, which wasn't enough to take care of me in school. Nonetheless, the joy and excitement of finally going to school outweighed the subtle reality of insufficient provisions.

So, I went to the dormitory to pack my stuff into my trunk. That night was a great night for me, indeed. As I buried myself in my sleeping cloth, my imagination took me to school, I wondered how life at the SHS was. As I pondered over a lot of coping mechanisms, my mind went to the dining hall. I began salivating as I imagined how good the food was going to taste. How did I know? My other siblings gave me a gist about how the food tasted so nice and how they never missed dinning.

As my mind was processing all of these, I saw a small mouse run towards my trunk which contained my numerous soaps and few other provisions. I flanged my pillow with all the strength in me at it, but it dodged and kept starring right at me. I timed it and quickly grabbed a book and threw it at it but too bad; the book hit the trunk so hard, causing some students to wake out of their sleep. We had a small lamp to give us light in the dormitory. I descended from my bed (I was sleeping on the top section of a two-tier bunk bed) and searched for this little mouse, but it finally escaped. Damn! This poor mouse was lucky, indeed. I would have squeezed the life out of it.

I climbed back to bed, awaiting daybreak, but strangely enough, that night was the longest night ever in my life. I kept tossing on the bed till the rising bell finally rang.

Later that day, I got some of the boys in the Home to escort me to the junction to get a bus to Koforidua, where my school was located. I couldn't believe it was indeed happening; I was on my way to school! Delay is indeed not denial, as often said. I greeted almost everyone I met on the way with a broad smile. And like magic, we covered the distance within a few minutes. As we walked on the footpath through the bush with birds flying all over and some rivers flowing gracefully down their path, I had no idea what was ahead of me. I could only hope for the best.

Upon arrival at the school that day, I expected to be taken to the boarding house, but no. Instead, I was admitted as a day student and made to lodge at the Body of Christ Baptist Chapel church's office (The church that founded the orphanage I grew up in). This made me a bit uncomfortable and scared at the same time, but all the same, I was happy I was finally in the SHS. Mosquitoes always invaded the room I was assigned to sleep in at the office. It looked as if the whole city's mosquitoes were sent there every night to torment me. No amount of mosquito repellent or spray could eradicate them. Throughout my stay there, I kept wrestling with mosquitoes every night. And guess what? I always was a loser as I lost my sleep daily.

## Food for thought

Not all care leavers get sponsors immediately to pursue higher studies after they leave the orphanage. Others never get any sponsor at all. I remember some of my siblings had to stay at the Home for over two years before getting the opportunity to go to SHS. Some also started but couldn't finish because the sponsors who were taking care of them halted their sponsorship. When this happens, they eventually are kicked out of the Home. Most times, these care leavers are not sacked directly but situations as these make living in the Home uncomfortable hence they are left with no option than to leave the orphanage to seek other means of survival (living with friends, close or distant relatives). This is one reason I commend a policy like the free SHS. With this policy in place, at least every care leaver can boast of a SHS Certificate.

At the Home I grew up in, our father made most of my siblings who couldn't get access to SHS re-register for the BECE when the free SHS policy was introduced in 2017; all 15 of those who passed are in the SHS. More of such social interventions are needed in our educational system.

# *Chapter 4*

## LIFE IN HIGH SCHOOL

*March 2008*

### My First Days in School

Dressed in my black and white attire since I was not given my uniforms then, I went straight to the general arts class on my first day as that was the course I was given. Fortunately, a different person (a male) also joined the class on that same day, which meant there were two new faces for the class to deal with so, I wasn't alone then. But surprisingly enough, not to me though, the whole class preferred my male counterpart to me, and no one came to say even a 'hi' to me. I felt terrible within. Perhaps I didn't have that charming look and didn't appear like I was from a wealthy home. I knew it because my school bag alone was another topic to discuss another time. If I remember, I sat in the same position the whole day until school was over; I never looked left, right, or back; it was only forward. This continued for several weeks. Most of my colleagues I contacted for their notes refused to give them to me for reasons I cannot tell to date.

I had to devise a means of catching up. I always sneaked in to take people's notebooks to the church's office, where I lodged as a day student and brought them back the next day. I would wait for the whole class to go for lunch and quickly place the book on their desks. I remember one girl who screamed out of shock when she saw her book, which had mysteriously disappeared from her bag the previous day and said a ghost had come for her book. She couldn't believe how the book she has been searching for just appeared on her desk. I only laughed out loud in my head and said, "I am the ghost! I am a ghost!"

Later that afternoon, on my way home to the church office—my dormitory, I felt lonely the whole time. Questions like, "why do my mates not like me?"

"When will these be over?" etc. kept running through my mind. I walked out of the school with several unanswered questions on my mind to the roadside and then picked a vehicle back to the church office.

I could not afford a variety of foods, so my food was always kenkey (a traditional Ghanaian dish made from fermented white corn) with pepper because I found it cheaper than other foods. Besides, it kept me full for a more extended period.

I remember one evening, after buying my normal ball of kenkey with fish, I slipped and fell in a gutter right in front of the church office. The kenkey flew out of my hand and landed straight inside the gutter full of wastewater. I was torn between removing the

41

kenkey from the gutter or going to sleep on an empty stomach. I chose the latter instead. As I watched the kenkey in the gutter, a droplet of tears fell from my eyes. I quickly wiped it off with the back of my hand and headed towards the office. I wished I could get someone to talk to, but no one was available at that time. I looked up and saw one biscuit I had bought the previous day lying on my books as I laid on my student mattress. I quickly pounced on it. I finished it within seconds and flushed it down with water and then soothed myself to sleep.

The next day in class, I asked for the previous term's notes from some of my classmates, but they blatantly refused. One girl had to cover her book with the blood of Jesus before handing it over to me. Oh, how I got to know that was what she said before handing it over to me was shocking.

The first teacher I had an early connection with was our social studies teacher. She was the only person who cared to ask why I had come to school late and where I was coming from. As early as 6am, I would leave the church's office to go to school to arrive early in class. This was my routine until after school one Friday when I met the senior housemistress. She notified me that there was a vacant bed in one of the houses, so I should bring my stuff on Monday. That was one of the beautiful moments of my early life in SHS.

As I walked out of the school to the roadside to pick a vehicle, I was in high spirits. I was grinning from ear to ear all along and didn't even bother about who was watching or not. I was so overjoyed. I got my fare paid by a good Samaritan in the taxi I picked. When we reached my destination, I leapt out of the car and said a heartfelt 'thank you' to this good Samaritan. I didn't ask for his name, but he was a young man in his late thirties and well looking as far as I can recall. His response was my dear, "don't mention it." I walked past the numerous people at the station and joined the busy road that led to my sleeping place. I could not just wait to get to the room to pack my stuff into my trunk.

At last, I was going to become a boarder. I relayed the news to our father back at the Home, and he was equally happy. I kept tossing over the weekend on my bed and dreaming about the new life I would live at the boarding house.

Monday came, and I finally said goodbye to my wrestling counterparts-the mosquitoes as my father at the Home came to take me to the school and dropped me off at the administration block with my trunk. When we arrived, he went to talk to the housemistress and then left. I didn't know what the discussions were all about, but their facial expressions gave them away as my housemistress kept nodding and showed a sign of concern with her mouth tucked in. I figured our father was narrating my ordeal to her.

I went to class that day after he had left and came back to the administration block after school as the housemistress had instructed. She got some big girls to help me with my trunk, and I was taken to Nyaniba House. However, I had to sleep in the annex because the main dormitory was full. That is how my life at the boarding house began. On our way to the dormitory, I couldn't look any student in the eye. The shoes and the wristwatches they were wearing made me feel belittled. Each question from them sent a chill down my spine as they spoke perfect English.

I responded with a yes or no, and much nodding's as I didn't want to disgrace myself. For those questions that demanded long answers I smiled them off, revealing my beautiful dentition as that was the only thing, I was proud of at that moment.

## Food for thought

It is often said that all the fingers are not equal, and no one knows tomorrow. Parents and guardians should endeavor to teach their wards at any level never to look down on anyone. In other words, moral values such as appreciating and accepting people no matter their race or status in life should be encouraged. Inferiority complex is one thing every care leaver battles with.

For instance, I battled with inferiority complex during my SHS days and while studying for my undergraduate degree. People wouldn't just associate with me simply because I did not have much and did not look or talk like them. I visited an orphanage in the Eastern part of Ghana some time ago and heard something that broke my heart. Some of their mates were mocking some of the children in SHS that came from the orphanage. How is that their fault? As a result, the orphanage in question had to pay for the services of some

IT gurus to hack into some websites to have these children's pictures deleted to allay any future mockery these younger ones are likely to face

Like most children who grew up in orphanages, I kept this orphanage fact to myself for many years as I feared I would be ridiculed. Most of the successful alumni from some orphanages I reached out to have their stories shared in this book declined as they wanted to hide their identity. They all were afraid of being looked down upon, but that shouldn't be the case.

# Chapter 5

## WAIT FOR IT

*April 2008*

I was shown a bed upon my arrival at the dormitory where I was to put my mattress. It was the upper part of a bunk bed. As I was unpacking my stuff, one of the seniors noticed I wasn't the regular student. So, she inquired whether I was about to establish a soap factory in the school. That was because my soaps were more than my other provisions combined. At that moment, I didn't know what befitting answer to give her, and so I just smiled and didn't hold it against her. Conceivably, she didn't know me and where I was coming from at the time.

Before that encounter, I learned never to pass negative comments about anyone I meet. This is because one unpleasant comment could break them. The other girls laughed loosely when she asked that question. I only giggled and let go. While they were all stunned by my demeanor, I was busily recollecting an old story a friend shared with me earlier. According to him, he once met his long-time lost friend. This friend in question, a lady had cut her hair revealing some patches on the head. But he decided to commend the lady for having a beautiful haircut instead. Later on, he found out that the lady had survived cancer, and her hair was now growing back. Supposing he had teased or castigated this friend, can you imagine the harm he would have caused? Think about it!

Do you now get the gravity of the whole situation? This story has been a reference point throughout my entire life: at worst, remain reticent when I don't have any positive comment to pass about someone else. In this vein, whenever I want to comment on a negative situation, I endeavor to sound upbeat and encouraging.

Later that evening, I went for dining. I was awed by the large crowd and felt a bit intimidated. As I settled at my table, I scanned around and saw people's designer bowls and cutlery. As a custom, one person always dished an equal proportion of food onto everyone's plate. Some requested for small portions while others requested for more. The food tasted good compared to the ones I had been eating back at the orphanage. At least I could get a piece of meat inside the meal with accompanying vegetables and fruits as well. To me, it was like the Last Supper.

As we advanced, while other students complained about the dining hall food, I was grateful for it and always ate without complaint throughout my stay in school. I knew where I was coming from. Take breakfast, for instance…we were served cereals such as tom brown, (a local Ghanaian dish), Hausa Koko (millet pudding), and the likes with bread— something I saw once in a blue moon during my time at the orphanage. What more could I ask for? I could only be grateful and enjoy myself.

A typical weekday at the boarding house began at about 4am with activities that marked the early morning duties. These comprised of washing, bed making, cleaning the area around our beds, and sweeping the entire dormitory. We then marched outside for morning assembly and then finally to class.

Meanwhile, I still did not have many friends in my class though I was now in the boarding house. I did not know why no one wanted me as a friend, but I understood recently that it was because of the way I looked. I always wore this morose and severe look, as if my head was the carrier of the whole world's problem. I discovered those looks in some recently found pictures of my days in the SHS, which I will share with you in this book's last pages.

One day in the dormitory, I  asked one of the girls to wait for me, so we go to dining together. She told me she was not going anywhere with me and even asked whether we came to school together. That broke me down. I only wanted a companion, but I did not know it was a crime to ask for one. Since then, I decided to play by my size and not to befriend anyone in the dormitory. I always walked alone.

I joined the Scripture Union and made few friends there. Not too close friends, though, but the ones one need for daily survival. My class had study groups, and I decided to join one. But the group members of the various groups always told me the groups were full. So, I decided to take my solitary studies seriously because I was already one full term and some months behind. I resorted to studying very hard during preps mainly. Then there was this upcoming class test in integrated science that I promised myself I would learn very well and beat the class. I did, and by Gods' grace, I topped the class. It was after I had excelled that my class mates started coming close to me. I then vowed to learn very hard because that was the only way to draw others closer. During preps, I will pull my desk to the very front of the class away from every noise and distraction.

With regards to my spiritual life, *Our Daily Manna* devotional booklet was my companion, as I always used it as a guide for my devotions. I followed through all other programs outlined in it, such as the scripture readings and the planned fasting and prayers. This was my routine throughout the years I spent in the SHS.

Gradually, the end of term exam drew near, signaling the end of the second term. The exam timetable was posted on the school's notice board, followed by revisions and then the exam itself. As expected, the school vacated after the exams, and we were all asked to go home the following day. So, early the next day, I packed my exam questions, books, and uniforms into my bag and sent the remaining items to the storeroom. Most students carried their entire belongings home because their parents either came for them or sent drivers to pick them up.

On the night of the vacation, I decided to go to the drying line area, and I saw many scrubbing brushes and pieces of soaps scattered all around. I picked them up as quickly as I could before anyone could see me. My heart was beating faster as I went about this for fear of being sighted by anyone. Thankfully, no one did. Well, to the best of my knowledge, nobody did.

I counted about 10 scrubbing brushes, and I was happy because there wasn't any back at the Home. I will be the first person to send them to the orphanage. As for the soaps, there was no way I was going to leave them because we took our baths without soap sometimes at the Home. I got a polybag and packed the soaps and scrubbing brushes into it.

That night before the vacation, I could not sleep. I imagined myself telling my other siblings back at the Home about my experience. As I kept tossing on my mattress, I drifted off into profound sleep and only woke up to the sound of the school's siren the next day. After cleaning my assigned plot, I quickly sent my items to the school's storeroom and set off to the Home. When I was exiting the compound, I passed by a lot of beautiful cars. I could hear screams such as "mummy, I've missed you. Daddy, I missed you." And what amazed me the most was when I saw an entire nuclear family coming to pick only one-person Home. To me, that was so strange. I could see younger siblings hugging their big sisters. I watched for a while and walked out of the school gate to the junction to get a loading taxi to the central station.

At the station, I boarded another bus heading to Suhum and alighted after Nankese in a town called Akote. That was where the road leading to the orphanage was. As I reluctantly jumped off the bus, I braced myself with my school bag while holding my polythene bag in the other hand. To make the journey more engaging, I started counting every step until I could count no more. With my head bowed, staring at the ground, I paid attention to every insect that winged to every bird that flew over me to every farm I saw along the road. I could number over 20 birds of different colors flapping their wings all around. They would perch on a tree and do some little pecking and fly again. One of the birds that caught my attention was this dark brown bird landed by a small pool of water. I got fascinated as it sipped the dirty water. I tried getting closer, but it flew away. Oops! It was scared I would harm it, but far from that.

After walking on the untarred road for about an hour and a half, I got to the orphanage—a home sweet home for me with so much in mind.

Due to the constant disputes my parents had subjected me to; I found solace at the orphanage. At least, I got to be among younger people like myself, where we talked and inspired one another. I could also get a hand to hold and pray together with and many other things.

As I approached the school, I heard the children screaming my name, "Madam Deborah." "Madam, Deborah!" Almost everyone came from their dormitories to catch a glimpse of me and run excitedly to help me convey my bag to the room. My heart ballooned, giving me that instant feeling of heroism. At last, I made it to SHS.

After the expected 'welcomes' and the exchange of pleasantries, I handed over the brushes to the girls' perfect for sharing amongst the students who were assigned to scrub the bathhouse. We mixed the soaps, and that became our bathing soap for the next three weeks.

Later in the day, I shared my experience with the kids, and everyone was happy. Well, as far as I knew, they were.

### Kitchen duties

The next day, we resorted to our routine by helping the matron cook for the students. That was the duty of the big girls as we were called. The Home had a modernized kitchen with a gas cooker, but we resorted to using firewood because the gas expenses could not be catered for by the Home due to limited income sources.

The smoke in the process of setting the fire for cooking always got into my eyes, drawing tears I did not intend to shed. Sometimes the effect still lingered on even in my sleep to the point where my eyes kept shedding tears in my sleep. Due to this, I resolved not to get involved in setting up the fire again. I did everything I could to avoid smoke whenever I went to assist in the kitchen. I would instead resort to sorting out the beans or washing of the cooking pot. Going to the kitchen was one way I got to learn how to cook. It was busy but not hard work, with good compensation, since we could clean out the leftovers in the big pots and swipe extra food.

After every day's work in the kitchen, I would go to the library to solve my exam questions, one subject at a time. Sometimes, as I spread the exam questions to look for answers to them, I got super excited. But those moments when the answers seem far away, I walked out of the library with much disappointment to the room to sleep my grief off. I knew people's parents would pay for them to go for vacation classes but not me, so I would go to the library the following day until I answered almost all the questions. On one of those days, as my brain began to give me up by wandering unnecessarily while my pen remained stacked in between my teeth, I chanced on one book on the shelf titled "Smoldering Charcoal." I quickly grabbed it out of curiosity and guess what I found: here was this beautiful wall gecko glued to the book. I got momentarily frightened and threw the book to the floor. "How did this wall gecko get to the library?" I wondered. I guessed it was more frightened than I was, and so within a few seconds, I saw it climb to the top corner of the library. It wagged its tail and finally disappeared through the window. I quickly packed my books and sped off the library as fast as my legs could carry me and told no one about my experience. I was done with the library for that day.

Later that evening, as I laid in bed, I found out that inasmuch as nature is beautiful, sometimes it has a way of making you lose your breath. In nature we observe growth and development in living things, contrasted with the static state of the vast majority of that which is man-made. That wall gecko nearly made me lose my breath. It is impressive, indeed. Oh, how I love nature.

**Food for thought:**

Considering the kind of treatment, I received from some of my mates at SHS, it is highly recommended that counseling sessions be held for care leavers in all levels of institutions. Such counseling sessions will help them accept who they are and adapt to changing situations. Individuals and other NGOs could take up this course. This could be done at least once or twice every semester. That way, the self confidence of care leavers is built.

Back then, during my senior high and university education, I used learning as a coping mechanism to overcome sadness, rejection, etc. I was always learning not because I loved to, but because that was the only way to bury my sorrows and get appreciated by the people around me. Although it helped, it did not do me too much good as I became cold-hearted in sharing my worries with others. I felt like nobody cared about me. Other care leavers might not use my coping strategy but might resort to doing something more terrible- the reason why counseling sessions should be arranged for care leavers in the various educational institutions.

# *Chapter 6*

## CHANGE IS HERE

*January 2009*

### The Days of Reckoning

As a custom, before we returned to school every new term, our father at the Home would usually call a meeting and share our terminal reports to us since the reports were sent to him directly from our various schools.

Our father, a husband and a father of four, is beardless, well-built, and dark in complexion. He oversees the Body of Christ Baptist Church in his capacity as a pastor. As we affectionately called her, his wife, Mama Gladys, is tall, curvy with a beautiful long hair that she always flaunts by holding it in a pony or leaving it freely on her head. Her round face was always a delight to watch from afar. I always stole a glance at her, mostly in church, and would quickly take my eyes off whenever she turned to look in my direction.

Almost every child in the Home ran to meet our father's car on the way even before he got to the school. He always had goodies to share with the children. On his arrival, he would hug the kids and share whatever goodies he brought with him. The kids always disappeared after receiving their goodies. Kids will do anything to get their delicacies out of your hands.

Our father always cherished our meeting times. He would advise and encourage us to take our studies seriously, keep praying, and keep believing in God. "God loves you but hates your sins" was one of his favorite concluding statements whenever he spoke to us.

When school reopened, you would get delighted when he called again to determine how much your fees was, implying you would be going to school. That particular second term, I was anxious to receive my terminal report from school, but it was delayed.

## Becoming Acquainted with School

Whenever schools resumed, those of us whose schools were in the Eastern Region (Eastern being one of the 16 regions in Ghana and the Region in which the orphanage is located) were given GHS20 (~$4) as feeding money for the entire term. Those outside the Eastern Region were given GHS30 (~$6). Each time I collected my GHS20, I would buy one sanitary towel, pomade, roll-on, and *Coreen* biscuit. I know you are doing the computations for me. After getting some basic stuff like soap, gari, and then luckily, Milo from the Home, I would add them to the items I had already purchased and then head back to school. I sometimes got to school with only

GHS1.50p on me for the whole term, the reason why I never took dining food provided by the school for granted, as missing it would mean starving. This was my routine until I completed high school.

When I got to school in the third term of the first year, I was in exuberance. As soon I got to the campus, I walked to the housemistress and registered and quickly headed to the storeroom for my mattress and other items I left behind and sent them to the dormitory. On my way to the dormitory, I made few eye contact with some of the students and noticed how happy they were. I could hear some of them talking about the excursions they went to and how much they enjoyed those moments. I heard another student telling her friend she would bring all the pictures to prep that evening to show them to her. I kept hearing many such stories, and as I began to increase my pace, something caught my attention. I looked closely and saw a man hugging one of the students affectionately with a little girl capturing that priceless moment on the camera. I figured immediately the man was her father.

My sadness was aggravated, and at that particular moment… I wished I received a hug too from my parents or guardian. I knew that was not possible, but my mind could not process that. I lowered my gaze as tears swelled up in my eyes, threatening to drop. This time, I managed to fight back the tears from falling and quickly climbed the staircase leading to the dormitory. As a custom for me, I always arranged my books under my bed first, and then spread my mattress on them and covered it with my blanket and then my white bedsheet. After sorting my books, I unpacked my other stuff into my trunk. From the corner of the room, I could see people unwrapping tins of milk, tins of sardine, cornflakes, etc. I only watched intermittently and took my eyes off.

Then in no time, the dining hall bell rang. I sprang up from my bed, grabbed my plate, and went straight to the dining hall. The boys always had this attitude of 'shying' girls from coming to the dining hall by clapping. So, in times like that, when you entered the dining hall as a girl, all the boys would applaud you. I received those ovations countless number of times; I can't even remember some. Other girls would retreat as soon as they heard the boys cheering, but not me. Instead, I would go to the extent of standing inside the dining hall and signaling with my hands asking them to clap the more. That was how far I could tolerate and overlook inconsiderate behavior to feed myself.

The following day in class, our Science teacher announced our positions in the class, and guess what…I placed fifth. I pinched myself in my head and said in my mind, … "that was a good start." Although I wanted to top the whole class, I applauded myself for placing $5^{th}$ (out of 55 students) the very term

I went to school, as it was a second term and in the second month. I got motivated to learn more.

More importantly, the third term was going to determine whether I would become a Science student or remain an Arts student. I decided to put in all my efforts to study harder that term. I learned in the dormitory, at preps, at dawn, and even in the dining hall. I wanted to be up there in class; also because by that way, people tended to come closer to me.

The term progressed peacefully without any snags, and soon, it also came to an end, and as usual, I went back to the orphanage. As per what had then become a routine for me, I went around to pick a few soaps and brushes thrown away and sent them to the Home.

**Food for thought**

It is recommended that individuals consider sponsoring the few items care leavers would need in school to live a comfortable life. Donors should not be focused on sending food items and clothing to orphans only when they are in the Home.

Back in the orphanage, I grew up in, some of my sisters at the SHS level fell into many needless relationships just because they needed to survive. As much as some of us can stand all the hardships life throws at us, other care leavers cannot, since we all have different genetic compositions. To some, hunger means sleeping around or doing anything just to get fed, and to others, hunger means self-control until the food arrives.

# *Chapter 7*

## BEYOND THE FIRST YEAR IN HIGH SCHOOL

*January 2010*

### Blessing in Disguise

After the first year, each student was to decide on what course they wanted to study. I planned to study science, so I went to the assistant headmaster and told him I wanted to be in the science class. He said the class was full. I could not bear to continue pleading as all my pleadings fell on deaf ears. Our assistant headmaster was well built and had rigid looks with a protruded belly that complemented his colossal figure. At that moment, I felt like deflating his belly with my little finger. I looked like David before him (he being Goliath) as he looked down on me. I stared in disbelief as he ignored me to talk to other students who had come to see him with their parents. Yes! I understood I did not have any teacher friend or influential person to take me to see the authorities or even speak on my behalf, but I felt he should have listened to me. He only said I could go to the agriculture science class if I wanted but not the general science class. When I realized my pleas would not amount to anything, I stormed out of his office and wandered about briefly. I stood in front of the administration block with my eyes fixed on the motto of the school "PRO PATRIA," meaning *For Our Fatherland,* wondering what to do next.

Having been left with no other choice, I picked my bag and went to the agriculture science class. We can be so sure of ourselves that we don't know there are some doors we shouldn't be entering. God does not only open doors; He shuts them too. Sometimes, He does very painfully. "This has to be one of those times," I thought. But knowing that did not lessen my pain. Later that term, a new student was admitted into the Science class. This reaffirmed my thought that protocol mattered. While all these thoughts were going on in my mind, it dawned on me that Agriculture Science was the only subject I had grade one (distinction) in during my BECE… "It could be a divine arrangement," I whispered. "Dear God, only You know the direction my steps are to go. I will trust You with them." As I entered the agriculture science class, I felt at peace, and a sense of joy filled my heart. I knew this was where I belonged.

In the Agric class, we were only three females among 35 males. Interesting!

On top of the discomfort created by this lopsided gender ratio, the class had most of the notorious boys in the school. But there seemed to be a flicker of blessing in the disparity and notoriety associated with my class; I had friends at last! O, did I say friends? O yes, I had some real friends, and other people who found some use in me. This was the catch: A lot of the girls in the home economics department liked most of the boys in my class. I used to send letters to some of the girls on behalf of the boys, and when it was examination time, my head was inundated with so many wishes from these girls to the boys, and vice versa. I was affectionately called DDT (Deborah Dzifah Tamakloe). So, you will often hear… "DDT, tell this guy that I wish him the best of luck,"…among others. I wondered if I wasn't part of the exam because I wasn't given any such wish. I was just a carrier. My acrimony notwithstanding, I always did well to pass on the wishes either before or after the exam. After all we were friends. Hmm.

Generally, exams in my school were always written under strict invigilation, but students would still be students…We had our ways of asking for help from one another in the exam hall. As the exams are ongoing, you would see some of the students positioned on their desks at a 45 degree angles and their neck all stacked out like giraffe. Some would also slant their answer sheets so the smart eyed students could read their answers. I was no exception, as I turned my answer sheet always to be copied. As far as we wouldn't be caught, we spoke undertone and went silent as soon as the invigilator looks in our direction. I recall one exciting time when some students' sitting positions were changed for more than five times before the exams time was up. This was because the invigilator suspected cheating and some malpractice among them. Their behaviors, facial expressions, and body language gave them out. Immediately after the exam was over, these affected students resorted to raining insults on the invigilators, with some threatening to pour urine on them. Threatening as it sounded, it was hilarious all the same. They never got to be executed anyway

Beyond the errands, I enjoyed the bond that existed between the boys and me. As per our distinctive natures, I was always the one sweeping the class as these guys won't clean. For my reward, I always received some tips and praise from them.

They also did not mind going any length to ensure I was okay. I vividly remember their having to suffer some punishment after they had jumped the school's wall one time to get me medication because I was not well. That was how far they could go for me. I still love them now even as I write this book as I used to back then. Those guys were lovely. I can say they were the best part of my life in SHS, and I thank God I never read any course other than agriculture science.

Part of the exciting moments I remember was what happened when one fell asleep in class: the person would wake up to find some of the class boys standing around him or her to watch if s(he) would fart…that sound crazy, right? These boys could also do a farting competition…oh my goodness! There was never any dull moment in class: from frustrating teachers to sometimes making them wanting to cry. Per the rules of the school, food was not supposed to leave the dining hall. Yet, my mates always broke that rule. This was because the dining hall prefect was in my class, so it was uncomplicated. We could smuggle a whole bag full of bread to class 'for party'. Most times, I would bring them poker cards from the Home to play. All of these made my life in SHS very exciting. I enjoyed every bit of the time with my mates.

**Food for thought:**

I believe it would be a laudable idea for sponsors of care leavers to go beyond just monetary sponsoring and probe further into the care leavers' wellbeing. If I have had someone to hold my hands to the school authorities, I would have been admitted into the science class, But the story was different for me. Notwithstanding, it is expedient to make the best out of whatever life presents to us.

Care leavers should always know that not every one of their plans will fall in line all the time. Understanding that if plan A doesn't work, plan B will may save them from many heartbreaks in life. Also, orphanage founders, caretakers, and sponsors should always look out for the interest of care leavers (their wellbeing, day to day happenings in their lives) than just leaving them to fate and chance.

# *Chapter 8*

## INDELIBLE MOMENTS

### When the Loved Ones Come Around

We had two visiting hours in a month. I did not pretty much fancy visiting hours in school because I hardly got someone visiting me. My mum did her best to visit once every term. Sometimes, I never received any visitor at all for the whole term. A day to visiting, all the phone booths and the call centers in the school get booked as students would be talking to their parents, telling them what they wanted, et cetera. Knowing very well; that I would receive just one visit or no visit at all for the term; I usually left the dormitory very early on visiting days. The gate to the dormitory area opened at 4am, so I typically left by 4:30am or 5am on such days for the class to study. I would stay there till after dining in the evening.

On those days too, the dining hall food tasted better than other days. The reason being that most students would not come to dining, so only a few tables would be served. Thus, less food was prepared. I made sure I went with my bowl to smuggle some of the dining food in times like this. I received most of my clapping from the boys on visiting days. Since most girls would be welcoming visitors and not come for dining, the few that went were teased away by the boys through their clapping. I sometimes got emotional, but I encouraged myself to eat what I could eat, smuggle what my little bowl could contain, and moved to the dormitory. Upon getting to the dormitory, I would quickly wash down and lie on my bed to sleep. However, it was hard to avoid the delicious aroma oozing from various homemade meals that were brought to my mates in the room. I could be on this inevitable humiliating aroma sampling spree till sleep takes over my poor olfactory system. I thank God for Nancy my friend. It was not all gloomy all the time; Nancy's mother would always bring me my own portion of food anytime she visited her. Although it felt a bit embarrassing, I did enjoy those moments as I got the opportunity to taste home meals.

## Worshipping God

Sundays were special days for me because of church service. Church service was held late afternoons and sometimes in the mornings. I always left my dormitory, dressed in my church costume to class, and study before going to church. During the service, I could dance to the hymns until I dropped. Hymns like *"Me Nyame aseda y3wode,"* meaning "*My God, to you be all the thanks,,"* was my favorite. It was compulsory to wear one's church cloth, and so the entire room looked wonderful as every student was adorned in their cloth. The chorus from the hymns we sang, I believe, reached the heavens directly without bend. Our voices blended so well with the piano that played in the background with every head pensively buried in a hymn book.

Ministrations from our school choir usually accompanied the collective singing of hymns. Our school choir was one of the best choirs in the whole of the Eastern Region. I remember they received invitations to several programs to sing and won a couple of awards. I wanted to join the school choir but lost the interest to do so due to the strictness of the choir master. Our Chaplain mostly delivered the sermon. After the sermon, we would drop our offerings in designated bowls, sing the closing hymn, and disperse to dining. Preps followed after dining. After preps, I would return to my dormitory to prepare for the week ahead.

Most times after preps, I would see a group of girls reading out letters under streetlights and laughing out loud. I assumed those letters were from their loved ones. During preps, I could sometimes see people coming with pictures and narrating to their friends where they spent their vacation. Much chinwags happened during prep. As the custom was for my school, girls were made to study in separate classrooms from the boys. We were never put together. I guess you know the reason.

**Food for thought:**

I think parents who visit their wards in boarding houses could arrange with housemistresses/masters to know the number of care leavers in their respective houses. That way, food prepared for their children could be doubled, and a portion served to these care leavers on visiting days.

# Chapter 9

## THE END UNFOLDING

*November 2010*

### The Award and Anniversary Ceremony

By the time we got to final year, I had already made a name for myself as one of the brilliant students of my class and the school as a whole. Before our final exam, there was a pending Speech and Prize Giving Day, which coincided with the school's 55th anniversary, and I was looking forward to winning an award. I did not know which award categories were available. All I did was to pray and learn.

As part of the celebrations' preparations, there was an interclass competition, and my class won. We scrubbed our desks, painted our blackboard, and made a mini notice board. It was one of the unforgettable moments in the class. Our class teacher was a good man; he supported us to win. He had this close look and was loved by all. He always wore a neatly trimmed beard and mustache.

Finally, the day of the anniversary came, I won two special awards in addition to what I was anticipating (Best Agricultural Science student award). They were the best debater's award, and the best public speaker award. Let me give you more gist:

There was this interclass debate competition in the school, and I competed on behalf of my class. I remember debating against the motion "cars don't kill; drivers do." It was very competitive, and I lost to one girl I trusted. She came to me to discuss the motion, and unknown to me, she was going to compete for their class. Eventually, she knew all of my points, so I lost. Nevertheless, I won the award.

To my amazement, the then headmaster of the orphanage I grew up in was present at the anniversary. He happened to be an old student. My mum was there too, and to date, I don't know how she found out because I do not remember telling her. Maybe it was just a coincidence: the durbar was held on a Saturday, which was a visiting day as well. So, she probably was on one of her irregular monthly visits. It was a great day in my life. When my name was mentioned for me to come for the award, I could hear the crowd cheering … "DDT! DDT!" The applause almost made me deaf. At that moment, my hands and legs began to shake, but I gathered the courage to walk on the artificial aisle to receive the award. I could hear and see the flashings and the shuttering sound of cameras all around me, and as I returned to my seat, there was my superwoman, my mum walking with pride to meet me. She was followed by the then headmaster of the Home school I earlier mentioned. They hugged me simultaneously. Words would fail me if I should try to describe that feeling. I felt like I was on a different planet…maybe Mars. My imaginative mood was activated as I imagined myself shaking hands with presidents of nations and other top dignitaries one day.

My thoughts were cut short as my mum, who noticed my mind wasn't with her at that moment, asked that I follow her to get the homemade meal she brought to me. As if she knew about the occasion. She brought me my favourite banku with okra soup. I took a few photos with her and went back to the dormitory, all hale, and hearty. And for the very first time in a very long time, I missed dinning. Yes, I did.

## Preparing for WASSCE

In the last term of our final year in school, we final year students were made to stay back in school during vacation whiles the other students went home. This was part of our final preparations; towards the West African Secondary School Certificate Examination

(WASSCE). I got a hint that any student who would obtain 8A's (*'A' represents excellent on the grading scale*) would win a scholarship to the tertiary institution. Armed with this information, I resolved to work harder to make the grades. To this end, I made a number of adjustment to my lifestyle to enable me soak in more.

I would usually eat very fast at the dining hall and sneak out even before dining is over to make time for my books. To me, the exam was a world cup and I had to prepare adequately to win the trophy ---my future depended on it. I invested all my time in learning. So committed was I to my books that I did not have time for a relationship. No one even approached me to ask me out except one guy who did, and when I turned him down, he told me I pushed him to propose to me. To date, I don't know what I did to make him propose to me. Consumed with my goal to make all A's, I was so much engrossed in my books; I had no time for any distraction. Some of my mates usually approached me during preps whenever they had challenges with specific questions, and I would help them solve them and proceed to offer further explanations if I had them. That selfless act helped me to know my shortcomings with some of the topics and helped me learn more.

Six months to the exams, all Agric. students were asked to drop Physics, which was one of our elective courses, and study Animal Husbandry instead. After studying Physics for almost three years, they changed it six months to WASSCE. We had no option than to put in our best. We had a visiting teacher from one other SHS to teach us, and he did his utmost. We did not have access to a lot of past questions since the subject was new. The days kept approaching. We counted down the days on our mini notice board in class as we all waited in anticipation of what lay ahead.

As part of the preparations towards the "world war", we wrote our first mock, second mock, and the third mock examinations. All my grades were concentrated around B2. That was encouraging as our class teacher told us that scoring a B2 in the mock exams meant an A in the WASSCE because our mock examination questions were more challenging than the WASSCE questions. I intensified my prayers and studied much more. I believe in the goodness and mercies of God. I always knew He was a prayer-answering God. I had a journal that I wrote indelible moments in. Writing in my journal was a daily routine for me. I always started my writings with 'Dear diary' if it has to do with new things I chanced on or 'Dear God,' for a specific need or request I needed answers for.

**Then WASSCE arrived**

*March 2011*

The D-day finally arrived. Our first paper was Oral English. I sat in the exam hall and did not even realize when the exam ended. All I could remember was: "What is the capital of Britain? London is the capital of Britain". I selected some possible objective answers and submitted the answer booklet. It was tough for me, especially because that was the first paper. After my abysmal performance in the first paper per my own assessment, I had to brace myself for the rest of the papers. For the rest of the papers, most students stacked their calculators with objective answers, while others memorized long objective answers. They claimed those were the answers. Memorizing objective answers did not work for me, so I always avoided them. I went to the exam hall in the mood of prayer all the time. Someway somehow, I never left any question unanswered. By God's special grace, I manoeuvred my way out of every difficult question.

Thankfully, the rest of the papers progressed hitch-free. My last paper was on the 18th of May 2011. After the exam, the school's gate was opened for students who would like to go out to do so and come before midnight. Most of my mates, especially the boys, ran outside of the gate bare-chested while waving their shirts in the air like some flag. Obviously, they were pleased, and that was the way of celebrating the accomplishment of successfully completing SHS. I preferred to go into a discussion with my maker or sleep, so I did not go outside that evening. With mixed thoughts running through my mind coupled with motley feelings, I went to the dormitory and knelt beside my bed with my head touching the bed and one hand holding my bible, thanking God for the strength granted me to go through the exam. I grabbed my hymn book and sang some of the hymns silently as I always did.

I stopped the singing at a point due to the loud discussions in the dormitory. What caught my attention was how most of my dormitory mates were sharing their after-school plans among themselves. Some said they were going to tertiary that same year. Others said they were going to travel abroad. Few students had teaching job offers to take up. Some even said they were going to do top-up courses. Others said they were going to write Nov/Dec, i.e., WASSCE for private candidates. I did not plan to continue with tertiary education that same year because I did not know where I would get the money for it. Besides, I did not know what was ahead of me. It was all hope! hope! and hope. They were tied to aspirations.

## What next after WASSCE?

*May 2011*

I packed every one of the few items I had and bid farewell to all my teachers, school daughters, and friends and left for the orphanage. As I sat in the troski that took me to the Home, my mind traveled into a faraway land where I saw myself going to the tertiary institution and having a lot of money. I came back to myself when the bus conductor screamed, "Young lady, I thought you said you would alight here. Please get down quickly." I said, "sorry" and stepped out of the bus, confused. I am sure the bus conductor was wondering what on earth it was that had gotten me so absent-minded. As I stopped at the junction organizing my stuff to embark on the journey-on-foot to the home, the thoughts kept running through my mind. Ahead of me was the long, seemingly unending dusty road to the Home. I walked haphazardly like a drunkard with no sense of direction.

I had high hopes to go to the tertiary institution, though none of the students in the batch before me at the Home were able to make it. They did not go because they had poor results but because there was not any help from anywhere. I prayed that my story would be different.

I went to the classroom to teach a week after I finished the WASSCE. I taught Science,

Akuapem Twi (a local Ghanaian language), and other subjects, depending on the class I handled at any point. The Home lacked teachers at that time due to its inability to pay them on time and so forth. Coupled with that, most of the teachers who came did not teach the kids well because they felt they were not being paid well. However, the few that taught the kids well had moved on. Some became medical doctors, immigration officers, soldiers, policemen and women, among others.

I did the teaching enthusiastically without taking any salary. I became extra loving to the kids. I washed for the younger and feeble ones on weekends and guided most of them whenever I had the time. I went around the dormitories to check on the sick students. I dressed the wounds of most of the kids and counseled them where necessary. On Sundays, I usually lent my dresses to some kids who did not have dresses to wear to church and took them back after church service. I went all out

95

to support the kids in my small way. On Sunday mornings, I would organize some of the students to clean the assembly hall for church service. I thought I was going to teach until my WASSCE results come, but a higher task awaited me. It was a position more significant and higher than my age, but I had to accept the challenge.

## Food for thought:

As part of their corporate social responsibilities, I think both large-, and small-scale businesses could consider engaging care leavers who have completed either SHS or are on vacation. This should come with some form of remuneration to enable them to cater for some of their essential needs. This way, the care leavers get to acquire some skills and earn some income to keep them going.

# *Chapter 10*

## POST HIGH SCHOOL

*June 2011*

### The Young and Ambitious Administrator

I was appointed as the administrator for the Home after a month of teaching. The teaching however did not stop. As the administrator, I had to serve as the acting headmistress in the absence of the headmaster. I had to welcome donors and other visitors on behalf of our father. I also had to plan our menu and ensured there were order and sanity in the Home I also had to supervise the teachers to do their work well.

Furthermore, I had to make sure I went with the kids to the mills to have our corn and cassava milled. I had to ensure there was enough firewood, fuel for the generator, etc. It was an enormous task as I was only 17 years old, but I realized I had that leadership skill in me one way or the other. You know sometimes new tasks and challenges come to reveal a new 'you.' It is in those moments you realize you have so much capacity veiled within.

I took up the task. I was given a phone to use so our father and any other person could reach me. That was the first phone I ever used. I listened to the radio and played music with it because being a dumbphone those were its other functions besides the main phone calls.

## Morning Worship

We had devotions every morning. Almost every child at the Home dreaded such moments because the early morning rising was not favorable to them at all but it made them stronger. You are sure to see some of the students wrapped in their sleeping clothes and standing aloof. They would neither sing nor clap all in an attempt to preserve their sleep but too bad for them as our devotion master always pulled the cloths off them and kept them until the devotions were over. Some boys who ran to hide in the bathrooms and the toilets to skip devotions were always caught. Some even went to the extent of hiding under their beds and faking illness. That was the extent to which some students hated to have their early morning sleep interrupted. Saturday devotions was the mother of all devotions as we stood longer than we did on other days --- from 4am to around 6:30am. Every child got to pray for themselves on Saturday morning devotions. The most annoying thing to the children was the announcements that were made right after the devotions. You are sure to hear some chuckles and murmurings. Most of these announcements were about visitors coming over or probably general cleaning. Everyone disperses to their rooms after the announcements to make their beds and off they went to sweep their assigned plots.

## Meals and Basic items at the Home

I had the keys to the storeroom and made sure no one went there without my permission.

After devotion in the mornings, I would call the store girls to the storeroom and measure out the day's meal: everything we would need from breakfast to supper.

Breakfast eaten at the Home was about ninety percent of the time, porridge, mostly without bread except during Christmas or Easter. For about ninety-nine percent of the time, lunch served was beans with red oil or *Frytol* (A brand of cooking oil) without any accompaniment like the usual ripe plantain that goes with beans in Ghana. Dinner was mostly rice or banku (a Ghanaian dish which is cooked by a proportionate mixture of fermented corn and cassava dough in hot water into a smooth, whitish paste). I would measure out all the ingredients that would be needed for these dishes and lock the storeroom.

On Saturdays, when the bell rang after morning devotion, it meant that soap is being shared. Everyone got a bar of soap, mostly *key soap* (a soap brand in Ghana purposely made for laundry). And this must last each person for the week--- for bathing and washing of clothes.

Every month, every girl of menstruating age got one toilet roll to use when the 'red lady' came visiting. On days where there were sanitary pads, each girl had about six pieces of the pad and a toilet roll.

Occasionally, you could see some of the students cracking nuts, chewing them, and smearing the residue on their skin as pomade since most did not have pomade most of the time.

I was also in charge of Wednesday services, during which I taught the kids new marching or worship songs. Sometimes, I would preach to them if there was no one available to do so. During vacations, the kids were grouped, and each group given a prayer topic to pray at a specific time. These were all done to keep the children busy at the Home and to help develop them spiritually.

As part of my duties as administrator, and in line with the modus operandi, students would notify me when visitors came in without prior knowledge. I would quickly run out of my office to welcome them and attend to their concerns. In situations where visitors would want to meet the students, I would get the students congregate at the assembly hall by having the bell rung to signal that call.

In the mornings, I would usually go to all the classes to check if they were all engaged. Anytime the kids heard I was approaching, classes which had apparently been noisy from a distant suddenly became mute. To keep idle classes busy, I would enter the class and write a class test on the board. Sometimes, I would ask them to recite the multiplication table, and if they were unable to do so, I would ask them to sit down and quickly learn it because there would be a class test. I had to use all the strategies I could think of to keep the kids busy.

I was in charge of the choir too. I taught them songs on Saturdays to sing on Sundays. I sometimes led the songs myself.

I had the busiest schedule ever. I was always the last to go to bed, as I had to ensure everyone was asleep. This was my routine for as long as I could think of until I left that office. I was enjoying my new position and the numerous activities until something happened.

## From Joy to Sorrow

An organization named Bridging the Information Gap built a computer laboratory for the Home. This place became the second Home to most kids after school because they all wanted to know more about Information

Communication Technology (ICT) and computers.

One fateful afternoon, our father came to the school and called me to the volunteers' quarters. We had volunteers' quarters which housed volunteers from Germany and other parts of the world. They were fed differently from the school's menu. Typically, most of the children were usually seen there as they went to play with these volunteers.

Now back to my story. Our father asked me to get someone to sleep at the volunteers' quarters because the last batch of volunteers had left, and the new batch was scheduled to come the following month. Due to the numerous activities on my mind, I forgot to ask some of the older students to sleep there. Coincidentally, our security man was not at his post that evening, either. That very night, the computer lab was robbed. What! I could not believe my ears and could not think of why I forgot to let someone sleep in the volunteers' quarters. The volunteers' block was opposite the computer lab, so having a handful of people sleeping there would have provided some security for the lab in the absence of the security man.

On his return, our father asked me if I carried out his instruction of getting some older students to sleep at the volunteers' quarters. I could not answer because I did not know what to say. The attacks then started coming. Most of the village folks came to the Home to vent their anger on me. Some said I was incompetent and questioned why such a position should be given to me. Maybe the post should have been given to them instead, I guess. It was a painful experience for me. I could not sleep well. With my pillow and handkerchief always soaked with tears and all the pain in my heart each day, I prayed for the thieves to be made out and the computers returned; that prayer is yet to be answered. Flickers of hope occasionally came in when some students came to me from time to time with accessories such as mouse, cables, claiming they found them in the cocoa farms nearby. My heart would skip with some hope at every new discovery. "Was that a sign that we would still find these culprits?" I thought to myself. "God is in his heaven, all's right with the world," I would shrug.

As I reflected on this very experience, it dawned on me that things happen for a reason. Most times, we get to know the reason later in life. Sometimes, the reasons are hidden from us for a lifetime. I wish I knew who the thieves were and where they took the items. I still remember the pain in my heart as I attempted to understand the reason why it happened. It all did not make sense to me. The more I tried to understand; the more my heartache was aggravated. So, you know what? I tried my best to leave it behind me and move on.

Then again, one child got admitted into the Home, and I was charged to keep an eye on him. Kofi Emma (Kofi means a male

Friday born) was very smallish in stature with tiny red patches on his face. The smallness of his stature made it easy for him to penetrate all sorts of crevices with ease. He always wore this sad face with which he deceived every one of us as he appeared vulnerable all the time.

This boy played the fool out of me. I will tell you why and how. About five percent of the students were not orphans, so they paid school fees. Their fees were used to run the day to day affairs of the Home. When these students came to pay school fees, I would keep the money and later send it to the bank after I got a sizable amount.

I realized that this particular new boy would come to the office, acting as if he was not well. He did this for several days. Unknown to me, he was monitoring me. One day, I returned from the mill with the kids to find the office door ajar and the locker where the money was kept open. As I tried to make meaning out of what had happened, some students came running to me with a complaint that Kofi Emma was missing from the school. My fear was confirmed after I searched for him in the dormitory and all over the compound. He had disappeared with the few Cedis I had saved for the school and the school's phone, which I was using. I could not control my tears. This boy had done me evil. We searched everywhere for him but to no avail. I sent some of the boys to the nearby towns to search for him, but he was not found. To date, I do not know where he is in the world. That was another hard pill to swallow. That night, I divorced my sleep and married my tears.

My pillow got soaked with sobbing. Those tears could water an entire garden. "Dear Lord, please comfort me," was what I could mutter. "Please comfort me," I muttered these words till sleep came back, befriending me unawares. That night I dreamt that Kofi Emma was standing at a faraway place and smiling mischievously at me. Did I say a smile?

It looked like he was making fun of me instead. I woke up, and my heart started beating like a sprinter on a marathon race. I held my breath since I could hear myself panting. It was in the middle of the night as I heard the crickets chirping. My eyes absentmindedly went to the far end of my room as I saw my shoes scattered at the entrance of the door. My eyes also located my jute sack with some of the clothing fighting for space into the bag while others struggled to fully enter the bag. The dilemma I was in did not allow me to fold my clothes. While tossing around and over the bed, I heard the rising bell ring. I hurriedly went to wake the children up for devotion as failure to do would mean zero attendance.

Later that day, I began to wonder and to connect the dots fully before the unfortunate incident. I realized that sometimes, people get close to you to gather information about you as much as they can and then strike you unawares. This type of attack can cause you much pain.

Beware and never assume everyone close is a friend.

Kofi Emma's incident happened one month after the computer lab was robbed. And there was always the bend in the road! The unfortunate incidences kept happening. Through it all, I never lost my praise and the power to pray. I kept praying and believing God for a turnaround.

While we were still trying to deal with the robbery issue, the unimaginable happened — we lost a student! That was the first of its kind in the Home. He was a sickle cell patient. It so happened that he wasn't getting better any longer within this particular period even after taking his medications, so we had to rush him to the hospital. I recall putting his head on my laps on our way to the hospital. I had that feeling to pray for him, but sorrows had overweighed my heart, and so I watched him but did not say a prayer for him. I left to pick some food items for the orphanage after the doctors came to examine him. The next day, our father called to inform me that we lost him.

At that point, I did not know what to do next. I gave up and cried my heart out. I felt like that was too much for me. Just within eight months of serving as the administrator, several misfortunes kept happening back-to-back. This time I went straight to my room and locked myself up and laid flat on the floor with no words coming out from my mouth. The more I tried to mutter some prayers; the more my mouth rejected those words. I understood Hannah's pain in the Holy Bible (1 Samuel 1 & 2) as her words gave her away due to the pain in her heart. At that moment, I wished an angel would appear to give me some words of encouragement, but no angel showed up. I had to become my own angel to encourage myself.

Finally, the day of the funeral came, and that was my first time seeing a corpse. I don't fancy the idea of funerals. I hate seeing people in a casket. Instead, I would love to remember them by the pleasant encounters we had while they were still alive and not in a coffin. I vividly remember how his name was called out three times at the cemetery, and at every mention, sand was thrown to cover him in the grave. It was a painful moment for me. When I think of the last moments of Godwin Gyenyame, when his head was on my laps, I did not know that was the last time I was going to see him alive. I came back after the funeral asking myself many questions. I quickly remembered one book I read titled *My Journey-Transforming, Dreams into Action*. In that book, the author A.P.J Abdul Karim said, "death is not something to be afraid of. Yet, the sadness that it brings cannot be shrugged away". We will go when our time comes, but when some of us go earlier than others like Godwin Gyenyame, who did not live to marry nor see his children, the sadness that surges up within the heart is a hard reality that one has to go on living with it. May his soul rest in peace!

## Shattered Dreams

I must say, amid all the chaos, I was still praying for 8A's simply because that would be the only way I would get a scholarship to enter into the tertiary institution. I declared all kinds of fast for myself: dry, wet, semi-wet, for three days, seven days, fourteen days, twenty-one days, you name them; just for my WASSCE results to turn out well.

Three months after the funeral of Godwin Gyenyame, our results were released. I gathered the courage to buy the WASSCE result checker, but I was hesitant to check it myself because I was afraid. I asked one of the teachers to check for me. He came back, laughing and smiling at the same time. In his words, I had done exceptionally well by getting 6A's and 2B's. To him, it was good news, one that called for a celebration. But I was indifferent: showing no sign of happiness at all. I was disappointed. Everyone around me was shocked because they expected me to jubilate instead. They did not know my plan. I did not know what God was doing, either. I questioned God and myself as to why I did not get all A's. Quite interestingly, I had dreams where I had all A's and that even motivated me to pray and fast more, but the 8A's only remained a dream.

But come to think of it, I suggest scholarship opportunities should not be tied only to excellent grades, but rather the givers of scholarships should pay attention to the beneficiaries' situations. For instance, a very needy student might not make all the A's but could get some good grades to take him or her to the tertiary institution. Do we neglect such a student all because they could not make all A's?

I had to change my prayer topic now. I prayed to God to release a helper instead because my 8A's agenda failed me woefully. I decided to take a step of faith first by purchasing the university admission forms… so I called my mum with one of the teacher's phone and asked her to help me get some money for the forms. She sent me some money which I think she borrowed, and I bought admission forms for two universities—the University of Ghana and the Kwame Nkrumah University of Science and Technology. I have always wanted to go to the latter, but God has a plan for each of his children, and those plans are always the best.

After I had submitted my application forms to the two universities, our father took me to several prominent people across the country to help me go to the university but no avail. I remember most of the offices we entered to date and the kind of chills that went through my spines. Notable among them was this highly influential top business woman. Before we were ushered into her presence, my courage had reduced to naught as the tiles and paintings, as well as the hangings on the wall, spoke volumes of her affluence and taste.

I became a stammerer when we were finally before her. My words failed to come out clearly. They hid in my throat like a thief running away from the law. I finally gathered all the courage in me since our father was expecting much from me. He signaled with his eye that I talk. I realized I was fumbling and shivering at the same time. I managed to mention my name to her as my eyes scanned her entire body. Her dress caught my attention, and I could not take my eyes off it. It was simple but classy.

She wore one beautiful designer watch with a lovely slippers and had her hair cut stylishly. At every click on her keyboard, my self-esteem diminished at the sight of her beautifully polished nails with a gold ring on one of her fingers. My eyes went down to my own ordinary and bare looking fingers. At that instance, I wished I had that ring on my finger too, including the laptop.

She then came in after I had struggled to introduce myself by mentioning my name, without credentials. She asked of my shoe size, and my face lit up instantly… I felt like screaming at the thought of getting new shoes. She again promised to buy me some other stuff, including new clothes. I could not wait to break the news to my siblings at the orphanage. I held onto those promises dearly, but alas, they never materialized to date. After the promises, she later advised me to apply for medicine in Cuba, but I read Agricultural Science, which certainly disqualified me. I went to an internet café the following day to check the Cuban website for any possible scholarship slot. To date, my inquiry of whether there was, and the means by which I could get a scholarship has received no response.

Over time, my hopes began to shatter, and the ultimate question was, how was I going to get the money to pay for my university education? Our father had done his best by taking me to all the people he felt could help me go to the university, but none of the people he took me to were willing to offer support.

**Food for thought**:

Stakeholders may want to consider dialogues where issues like the education of care leavers are discussed, and useful conclusions are drawn. I was the only person in my year batch to make it to the tertiary level, not because my other siblings never did well. They were equally qualified to have made it.

Also, individuals and organizations who institute awards and scholarship schemes should consider opening up and focusing more on students who genuinely need help such as care leavers and not only those who produce the best /excellent grades. That way, care leavers would benefit more.

In my case, although I managed to get 6As in the WASSCE, I wasn't even recognized or considered eligible for any scholarship, but heaven knows the kind of effort I put into studying to acquire the grades I had. There should be more rewarding platforms for care

leavers who make good grades despite the
problems they face.

## *Chapter 11*

## LIFE IN THE UNIVERSITY

*July 2012*

### A Step into the University

After weeks of waiting, I heard that the admission lists for the University of Ghana were in, but my name wasn't on any of the lists. I decided to follow up. I mustered courage and, in the company of a cousin, went to the campus of University of Ghana to inquire why my name was not on any of the admission lists. Well, I did not know what I was going to do on campus, but somehow, I had this inner feeling to pursue my due. All I had was my results slip. At the registry, my cousin waited at the entrance while I entered. I remember joining a long queue with prominent persons holding brown envelopes, suitcases, etc. who had come with their children. The queue kept moving, and finally, it got to my turn.

I entered, showed my results to the officer in charge, and told him that I hadn't seen my name on the admission list. The officer beamed with smiles to look courteous and welcoming, but the stress on his face gave him away. He doubted my story after seeing the results. He then asked me to go home with a promise to work things out, which I believed. When I stepped out of the Registry, a friend called to inform me that my name was included in the students' list admitted for the Agriculture Science course. By then, I had misplaced my placement voucher, so I did not know how to download and print my admission letter. I searched everywhere for it to no avail. I was then asked to check my text messages and that the university would send one. It never came.

Some days later, I found the voucher, but I did not have the pin. Thankfully, I had an option that permitted me to reset it. Having laid hand on the voucher, I headed straight to an internet café and met an accommodating gentleman as he assisted me with all the technical challenges I faced. I left the café with my admission letter printed in my hands. Everything was turning around for my good.


## The Turning Point

I had had my entry pass (admission letter) to the University of Ghana, thanks be to God. Then came the countdown to the closure of registration (confirmation of acceptance of admission). As at three weeks for the closure of admissions no helper had shown up; not even a promise. I was always lost in my thoughts and lost appetite. My mind was consumed with one question: "How was I going to get funding for my university education?". I found no answer, and I was beginning to lose hope of ever having a university education.

One afternoon after I had given up altogether on that ambition, my former Science teacher at the Home called through one of the teachers to enquire about how I was doing. Momentarily, I felt like telling the teacher to send the phone away as I wasn't ready for any conversation, but something within me prompted me to answer the call and talk to her. So I spoke to her, reluctantly though.

In the middle of our conversation, she asked about how things were with me and whether my results were good enough to get me admitted into the university. I told her the results were excellent, and that I had been admitted by the University of Ghana, but I did not have anyone to help me. She then asked me to write a scholarship application letter, attach my results and admission letter to it and come to her place at Korle-bu Medical School in Accra the following day.

That evening, I asked our father for permission to go to the Korle-Bu Medical School campus the next day. As to how I got the money for transportation, I do not remember.

How I managed to locate her campus is another whole book to be written someday.

My former science teacher was studying medicine at the time. She gave me such an unforgettable welcome. I spent a few days with her. In fact, at the time I got to this very portion of writing this book, I had to pause to post her picture on my WhatsApp status as my woman crush before I continued writing. She is a medical doctor now. She is Dr. Vanessa Omaro. God bless you Doc.

Indeed, God works in mysterious ways: ways far above human understanding, far beyond what the eye can see and what the heart can comprehend. She told me she had a pastor friend serving under a senior pastor who gives scholarships to underprivileged students, and that she would therefore have a discussion with him about my situation.

True to her word, she invited the pastor into her hostel, and after their discussion, the pastor and I went to see the senior pastor in question the next day, a Sunday. In the course of the service, I wasn't focused on anything. I don't even recall what sermon was preached that day. I had only one agenda, and that agenda was to go to school. After the service, I went into a private meeting with the senior pastor and my mediator pastor. Upon seeing me and glancing through my results, without any hesitation conferred the scholarship on me. Just like that! Yes, just like that. He then asked me if I had a phone. I responded in the affirmative though I did not have one at the time.

Truth be told, I did not believe what the pastor said. Of course, I did not believe in it because there was neither interview nor any background check, and besides, other prominent people I had met earlier given me so much hope had ended up disappointing me. I had therefore been conditioned, due to disappointments in the past not to bank on promises of people.

What made me doubt him the more was the simplicity of his outlook. He was not adorned in any fancy clothing; he wore a simple suit. You see, I was making judgments based on his looks following what I saw at other places I visited in my search for a helper. I understood later never to judge a book by its cover!

My skepticism notwithstanding, I decided to clutch to the little hope that came through for reasons I could not tell. Perhaps because he bore the title of "Man of God". I went back to the Home with that little hope to prepare for school. The countdown continued. As at three days away from closure of registration which would seal off my admission, my little hope had not yielded any results; I had not got money for fees. With no help to look to, I had to feign oblivion to my mum's financial position and fall on her for help I asked her to lend me some money and she did. She managed to get me GHS400 (~$80) from friends leaving a balance of GHS 233 (~ $40) to be added up.

While thinking through it in the washroom the next day, a name flashed through my mind, and that was the orphanage driver. I called him immediately I stepped out of the washroom and told him I needed GHS300 to pay my school fees with a promise to pay him back. He agreed, on the condition that I pay him the following Monday. I consented, and he brought the money to me.

With the full fees now in hand, I called Dr. Vanessa Omaro and informed her I was coming to her place. I packed up and left the orphanage to Korle-Bu. How I managed to have my luggage carried along is yet another story to be told another time. Upon my arrival at her hostel, she introduced me to her medical school friends and mates. It was a nice feeling. I shared the bed with her for a week, ate her food, drank her water, among many others.

I went to the university campus the next day to pay for my tuition and applied for a hall of residence on campus.

## The Arrival of the Guardian Angel

*August 2012*

I captioned this section as such because I believe there is an angel in a human form for everybody. I met mine at the time I needed him most, at a time I had given up on myself, and when all my plans were failing me.

On the first Sunday; after going to the University of Ghana campus, I returned to the church of my would-be-sponsor with my mediator pastor. As did happen on my maiden visit, I wasn't paying attention to the sermon. I do not recollect the songs that were sang nor do I remember anything that was said and done in the auditorium but my praying for the pastor to locate me, and indeed, he did dig me out: he called me out in the middle of the service, and that call I did not miss! It actually sent a shocking impulse through my body. I toddled forward and he handed me GHS700 right there in the service to pay my school fees. This was enough to pay my debt and pay for the new hall I had applied for. The pastor is Prophet Bernard El-Bernard Nelson Eshun, Executive Pastor and General Overseer of Spiritlife Revival Ministries headquartered in Accra-Ghana.

The following Monday, I finalized the registration, got my room keys, and went back to Korle-Bu. Dr. Vanessa Omaro bought me some provisions and gave me additional GHS300 for my upkeep. She got a taxi driver to send me to campus. On my way to campus while in the taxi, I just could not hide my joy. I was beaming with smiles throughout the journey... Was this happening? Wait! It was hard to believe... I was actually on my way to the university, and I could not wait to explore the new life ahead of me—the university life. I had heard many stories about universities and how most of the students lived loosely concerning letting their guards down on issues of morality especially. As I mused over these thoughts, my mum's earlier advice came to mind. She had called sometime back to lecture me on happenings at the university. She even sounded like she had schooled in all the universities in Ghana.

Oh mothers… and scuttlebutts. That makes mothers interesting, nonetheless. Having been armed with all the etiquettes, from my mum and friends, be they the truth or tittle-tattles, I was very determined never to go errant.

I finally arrived on the University of Ghana-Legon campus. I gallantly stepped out of the taxi in my old-fashioned hairstyle but with a bright face. I felt like everybody should congratulate me as I had come a long way. I went straight to the porters for my room key having 'fulfilled all righteousness' regarding registration. He gave me the key and said, "welcome." I responded, "thank you," feeling like a superstar. I went to my allocated room and met a lady who introduced herself as Rachael Commey, my roommate. Before I got to the room, my other roommates had come to select their beds already, so Rachael told me the last bed (the upper of a bunk bed) was the only bed not occupied by anyone. As if I cared about the bed! All I cared about was that I finally made it to the university. I nodded to all the long talks Rachael gave me and climbed my bed to dress it with my bedsheet. I did not have a laptop. Neither did I have a smartphone. All I had was an iron which I took from the Home, a rice cooker my sister gave me and a dumbphone my mum gave me. I made my bed and arranged my stuff. I went to the department the following day to do my manual registration.

Later, when the semester commenced, I made a few more friends. After the first semester ended, I went back to the orphanage to teach the children. Everyone was happy to see me. My eyes had opened to the new stuff: a novel way of talking, thinking, behaving, you name it.

Throughout my stay in school, I always sent a ''thank you'' note to Prophet Bernard at the end of every semester, whiles updating him with the next semester's fees with my results attached.

## Hustling to Survive

After the first year, I made new friends who always reported back to school early whenever we resume from holidays. I constantly went to school early and stayed with them on campus while waiting for my school fees. Prophet Bernard constantly gave me money for my upkeep, apart from the school fees. I would go back to Prophet Bernard when I ran out of cash, and he would refill my purse. I eventually joined his church and became a chorister to date.

Going to see Prophet Bernard in the church was hard for me because of the long queue I had to join and the numerous eyes that looked at me when I stretched my hands to receive the money from him. Sometimes, after I had gone to him for money, I would wish the earth opened up, so I could bury myself inside. At times, my neck became stiff as I left his presence with the money he had given me in my hands. I would be torn between laughing for receiving the money or frowning at the numerous prying eyes that fixed their gazes on me; and whether to greet the people I met on the way back or not greet them. It had always been a long difficult walk from Prophet Bernard's office to the forecourt of the church. I preferred him calling me than taking the initiative to go to him on my own. So, in instances that he called me himself to come for money, my joy knew no bounds.

One Sunday, when I was going to see Prophet Bernard for some money, one lady tapped me from behind in the queue and said, "as for you, you always go for money from Prophet Bernard." At that moment, I wanted to ask her how that was her problem. I didn't.

"Is it her money?" I inaudibly quizzed.

"Why can't people just mind their own business in this world?" " While all of these thoughts were playing in my head, I eyed her hard in my head but smiled on the outside.

After that incident, I vowed never to go for upkeep money again except for my school fees. This meant I had to hustle to get cash to feed myself. Sometimes in life, the things people say to you will either break you, crush your spirit, or push you to the next level. Always go for the latter.

I started applying for data collection jobs, and God being so good, I got one with the Hunger Project and International Labor Organization (ILO). This helped me make some money to save and cater for my basic needs. Although the data collection job wasn't frequent, I managed the little I got till the semester ended.

In my first year at the university, I was one of the first 10 students in the Agriculture Science Department to be asked to go for an interview for a particular scholarship. I declined the offer because I was already on one (Prophet Bernard el Bernard Nelson Eshun Scholarship Scheme). Maybe I shouldn't have!

## No Money, No Food.

My food on campus lacked variety. It was either beans stew or light soup due to lack of funds to go for other options. I went for the former because I did not have to add much meat and the latter because I only needed a few ingredients to make it enjoyable. I had to eat banku with pepper without fish countless times and beans stew without fish multiple times. But through thick and thin, I never gave up on my studies.

Later, I got introduced to the Bernard Nelson Campus Ministry, and I joined. I became friends with the campus ministry's president, and he has been one of my economic pillars to date. Dr. Vanessa also supported me whenever the need arose. As at my third year, I still did not have a laptop or a smartphone. Sometimes, when situations got more challenging, all I did was to pray. That was how I was raised. My life revolved around church and books, to-and-fro.

At a point, I felt like I did not fit in with the friends I had as almost all my SHS mates got admitted into the Kwame Nkrumah University of Science and Technology. The situation was worse in the church—I had no friends there either. We used to have morning and evening services on Sundays. On most occasions, wherever I would sit during the morning service was the same place where I would be throughout until evening service. I always had my books with me anytime, anywhere, so I read anyhow and anywhere.

Sometimes, I would go to the Accra Technical University (ATU) campus to study after the morning service. My church used to hold service at the National Theater, which was close to the ATU. So, usually, on some Sundays after the morning service and choir rehearsals, I would quickly go to ATU to study before the evening service. One Sunday, during one of my study times at ATU, I met a gentleman who later became my friend.

This particular gentleman of a friend was so good to me. He used to bring me provisions, and even when it was time for me to write my dissertation, he printed all questionnaires for data collection for me at his own cost. God sometimes brings people our way to be of help to us for just a particular period. After completing his assigned task, I lost touch with him. His kind gestures however remain in my heart. God bless him!

I am grateful to God that I later got some really good friends who fed me most of the time. I remember the day I prepared stew with chicken; all my roommates surrounded me and made me feel like I had won some presidential award. That day after I finished cooking, each of them wanted to have a taste of my cuisine.

## My First Award

*October 2015*

My grades were satisfactory after the first year, and by the grace of God, I managed to maintain good results throughout the remaining years consistently. This made me proud and happy. After all, that's the area I could also pride myself in.

Thus, it came as no surprise to me when I was informed I had won an award in my third year. That was my first ever award. I was given the *Akuamoah Boateng's best female level 300 crop science student award*. It was a delightful privilege. Out of excitement, I told my roommate about my award and asked her to escort me to receive it. When we got to the award center, I was called to receive my prize, a cheque sealed in a white envelope. I did not know how much it was. My roommate had a friend who picked us up at the award venue back to the hall. I got to the room, opened my bag in an ecstatic mood but, alas!

The cheque was nowhere to be found. What! That was not happening. I went back searching for it but could not find it. I called the guy who won the male category of the award and asked how much the cheque was, and he mentioned GHS1,100. My heart missed a beat! There and spontaneously, I promised to give God 20% of the amount if He helped me find the cheque. I came to the room with a sad spirit and countenance. All my prayer was for God to help me locate this cheque. I could not hold back my tears as they flowed freely down my cheeks while I wiped them with the back of my hands till I blubbered myself to sleep.

The next day, I went to report the incident to the Accountant at the student account office, and he told me all they could do was cancel the cheque and issue a new one when I return the old one. I was thrown into a quandary and a typical catch-22 situation. Where was I going to find the old cheque to enable me to get the new one? I went blank at that moment as it seemed I had lost the money for good.

A week later, I received a strange call. It was an invitation to come to the Crop Science department of the School of Agriculture. When I entered the office, I met a lecturer from the department who congratulated me on winning the award and handed over the old cheque to me. He told me a good Samaritan brought the cheque to him. He asked me about whom I went with to receive the prize. When I told him, he only giggled and cautioned me to always go to such functions with grown-ups to avoid any such lousy incidence from recurring.

My joy has been restored. I expressed gratitude to him, and I went straight to the account's office with it so that a new one could be reissued to me. As soon as I got the new cheque and headed towards the bank to cash it out, a tall list of needs started crowding my mind. I imagined buying myself a new phone. Or should I buy a new pair of sandals and some clothing instead? I was fascinated by my imaginations, and when I finally cashed out the money, I gave God what I promised Him, saved half of it and used the rest for my basic needs.

## The Final Days in The University

Time, they say, flies so fast than the speed of light. All too soon, three years had passed so quickly than imagined, and I found myself in my fourth and final year, Level 400 (L400). I had firmly resolved to write an outstanding dissertation and graduate with a first-class honors.

For my dissertation, I settled on a research that looked at the yield of cocoa farmers' in farmer based associations and those who weren't. I chose to do my data collection in the towns surrounding the orphanage to get a place to sleep and food to eat. My sample size was 60, and I was to select 15 respondents each from four communities in the district (Suum Kraboa Coaltar District). I dedicated a whole week to the data collection with the help of an extension officer.

I started analyzing the data right away as soon as I got back to campus from the town. By then, I had got an old laptop from the campus ministry's president, Danny. He asked me to use it to write my dissertation and return it when I finished. That was my first time owning a laptop, at least temporarily. It felt so good, although it was slow. I was bent on making my supervisor proud of my dissertation.

I rehearsed for almost two weeks towards my upcoming dissertation proposal defense. During the proposal presentation, I got the loudest applause signifying how well I presented. That made me gain the admiration of my peers and most of the other students. I started working on chapters one to three. The dissertation had five chapters in all. I decided not to go to the Home during the first-semester vacation of L400. I stayed over on campus so I could finish my dissertation early.

## Robbed at Knifepoint!

*January 2016*

In the first week when school reopened for the final semester in L400, Prophet Bernard called me to come for my fees. Anytime I went to his house, I wished the earth would open and swallow me. I was so shy of him, especially his wife. But honestly, they are amazing people.

After I had gone for the money from him, I went straight to the bank to pay my fees and came to the porter's lodge to take my room key. But the Porter on duty that day refused and demanded that I register with the hall the following day before he could hand over the key to me. I informed him I had paid everything and promised to finish the registration the next day. Yet he insisted, so I went back to the former room in the hall where I lodged during the holidays…only to be awakened from my sleep by a strange noise and presence in the room.

I opened my eyes to a knife pointed at me…It was around 3:30am … I got so scared to the bone as the reality of what was happening finally hit me—I was being robbed at knifepoint. The robbers came through the backdoor using the balcony. I could not believe what I saw with my eyes. My laptop and my friends own were all taken.

After taking the laptops, they pointed the knife at me again and ordered me to bring all my money. Prophet Bernard had given me some money for upkeep too. Unknowingly, they had already taken it and were asking me for more. As I looked for the money in the bag, I could not find it only for me to lower my head down and saw my money in the hands of one of them. I wished I could shout, but there was no strength in me. I pleaded with them, and they jumped off through the balcony, all the time signaling that I keep mute else I would be stabbed. Everything was like a movie to me.

That night before I slept, I read the first twelve chapters of Isaiah and prayed alongside those scriptures I read. After I was done praying, I felt I should relocate from my bed to the topmost bed in the corner of the room as the mattress looked very colorful. So, I left the laptops on my bed and jumped off to the new bed and dozed off around 12:30am. That was how my God delivered me as I would have probably been killed or raped if I slept on the beds the laptops were on.

At times, when these robbers are sentenced to life imprisonment, many feel sorry for them. But, when you fall victim to their unscrupulous attacks, you will appreciate such judgments better. These robbers did not know my story. They did not even care about how I was going to feed. They did not care about how I was going to finish my dissertation. Neither did they know how I even got the laptop and my friend's own too in the first place—I only asked my friend to allow me to copy a document onto her laptop because mine was messing up, and that was how I ended up with two laptops at the time.

I did not know how to break the news to the owners of the laptops…But for how long could I hold on to such information? I finally mustered the courage and told them. Guess their reactions…they did not say anything. I was shocked, and their non-reaction troubled me a great deal. I felt terrible and still feel bad about it even as I write this book. I was asked to report the case to the police. I did, and they arrested a suspect, but I later realized it was just a waste of time, so I stopped following up. The suspect was one of the garbage collectors in my hall who was transferred later to a different hall.

After the incident, I had to look for an alternative means to finish my dissertation. So, I resorted to using the department's computer laboratory to type, after which I would save it on my pen drive. Sometimes when I got to the room, I would use my other roommate's laptop when she was asleep. All my three roommates had laptops. Joana was a pharmacy student and mostly out of the room. Jessica was always watching a movie on her laptop and, Rachael, although busy, would ask me to use hers whenever I needed it. She was such a beautiful soul.

I managed to pull through and ultimately submitted the final thesis. We had written our final exam too, and so I was awaiting graduation.

Before the graduation, however, I discovered that my GPA was 0.01 short of First-Class Honors, leaving me with a Second-Class Honors instead. I was disappointed in myself. I wanted to make Prophet Bernard and my friends proud with a First Class Honors. Most importantly, I wanted to be proud of myself! But it did not happen. I felt I had disappointed everyone.

During graduation, I did not invite anyone except Martha, my cousin, who had earlier escorted me to the University of Ghana when I had a problem with my admission. My friend, Ephia Biney, made me up. It was a good day, but I wasn't happy. I was sneezing all through because I had a cold from the tears I shed the previous day. It was a bad feeling. My shoe was a little inch longer than my feet and that altered my stride. My feet kept slipping out making all those behind me bypassed me, probably because I was delaying. As I shook hands with the Vice-chancellor and the other dignitaries, I still did not feel great within as I was looking for a standing ovation from them. Standing ovation was the preserve of first class students. Alas, I was not a first class student. That was a very painful experience considering that I had worked so hard through thick and thin, and had come so close. 0.01 points away from the mark was just too hard to bear. What could I do? I had to find consolation in my having made it to the end at least despite the hopelessness from the onset and the challenges through the journey, and move on.

## National Service

*September 2016*

I had earlier applied to serve as a university teaching assistant for my national service. National Service in Ghana is a one-year program where graduates are posted to work with different organizations to help build the nation. Before the Secretariat released the names and locations for national service personnel, I already knew where I was going to serve. Thus, after going through the robust registration from waking up at dawn to joining long queues among other procedures, I started my national service as a teaching assistant. I struggled with getting a place to stay because I was no longer a student. I finally met a friend who was also in the same boat as I was. We put our little resources together to buy a bed from a continuing student. We shared the bed until national service was over. It was not an uncommon practice that most students sold off their beds at a higher rate than they had acquired them to students who needed them desperately. This the sellers did to pay their fees or sort other stuff out. Such sellers would then end up perching with others. It was illegal but trending during my days at the university.

## The Birth of Charis Touch Foundation

*August 2016*

During my national service period, I decided to set up a foundation to help care leavers, orphans, and other vulnerable children. I have been in the same situation as them and can comprehend their issues better. Motivated by this vision, I gathered some money from one data collection work I did worth GHS500 and with the help of two partners; Doris Narki Tetteh and Celestina Danso Arhin, legally registered the foundation in August 2016.

The year 2016 also marked the period of self-evaluation for me, where I forgave anyone who had hurt me and whispered "no more sheets" to my past life of pain, bitterness, and shame. *"No more sheets"* is the title of one of my favorite books by the American gospel singer, author, and pastor Juanita Bynum. I realized that to represent my other siblings back at the Home where I grew up as well as care leavers globally, I needed to be bold, reliable, and outspoken. If there was anything I did not believe in, it was self-pity. I still have a pretty cold, detached attitude about my own life—my daily dramas. But if you want to see me get emotional, talk to me about the people I love most—care leavers, orphans, and vulnerable children (OVC).

I started with the little outreaches: raising funds from friends and family. Our first outreach was at the orphanage I grew up in, BASCO. I got people on board to buy pairs of sandals and shoes for all the girls. I had a few clothing items. A team of supporters came along to help with distributing the freebies. The world was opening new doors to me. I started meeting friends, partners, volunteers, and many others.

**Food for thought**:

It takes a bit of sacrifice to make the lives of others better. It is highly recommended that individuals consider going out of their way to be of a blessing to care leavers. My teacher, who connected me to the Pastor, did not have everything. She was still a student at the University of Ghana Medical School. However, she sacrificed her little comfort to get me to where I am right now. Instead of waiting to get it all together before reaching out to others, we could begin to do the little things to help others and society.

Also, care leavers should do well to inculcate a saving culture and not squander everything that comes their way with the hope of getting more. I had in mind what I wanted for myself and so started saving a percentage of my national service allowances. This helped me pay almost 60% of my tuition when I gained admission to read my masters (details in the next chapter). Saving such an amount did not come on a silver platter: there were days that I had to sleep on an empty stomach. Care leavers should know that no one else will stand for them until they stand up for themselves.

Financial institutions should also take it upon themselves to reach out to orphans in care homes to provide some form of education to conscientise students on the importance of developing a saving habit before they leave the care homes. Furthermore, insurance companies can take it upon themselves to insure some young children in the various orphanages on their educational policies. They can do this in partnership with donors and other philanthropists.

# *Chapter 12*

## PURSUING FURTHER STUDIES

### The Dreams

*August 2017*

As the one-year national service gradually drew to a close, I began to have several thoughts about exactly what to do next. I decided to further my education, so I applied for schools outside Ghana and the University of Ghana for my master's program. Though I managed to save some money from my data collection jobs and my national service allowance, it still wasn't enough to pay my fees here in Ghana. So, all my prayers were for God to open a door for me to pursue my master's degree elsewhere with full funding.

Prophet Bernard's scholarship scheme had ended with the completion of my first degree program, and there was no promise of sponsorship for a second degree from any benefactor. I kept praying and asking for God's provisions. A while after putting in the application, the University of Ghana invited me for an interview. I got excited at the invitation and decided to give it a perfect shot. I looked through my clothes and selected a pair of black shoes and my favorite black skirt and gave it some really good ironing. I was in the highest of spirits. As I hanged the clothes, it looked so straight and neatly ironed and sharp as though the edges could cut through human flesh. That evening, I did tons of research…books were knocking on each other with pages flipping loudly. The internet wasn't spared either as I searched from Google and other useful resources and made notes. After I had gotten my brain exhausted with all the necessary tips, I went outside for fresh air. I walked around the field and watched as many students gathered to pray. Others stood on the field, chatting and giggling. I inhaled some fresh air as I imagined how I would answer the interview questions I was going to be asked.

After a long walk, I hurried back to the room to catch some sleep. That night I saw myself getting admission and pursuing my masters in my dream. I woke up with a thankful heart and dressed up for the interview. At the interview, each student was made to sit on a solo seat. I called it the hot seat. As soon as it got to my turn, I began shivering but acted all bold and confident. Questions were flying all over the room from the panelists to me. I managed to answer the questions brilliantly except for this particular one, which I could not respond to satisfactorily…I was asked to define an "identity matrix." After the interview, I was notified by one of the schools I applied for outside Ghana, but the message ruined my day. I was offered a partial scholarship, and I needed to raise an additional CAD5,000.

A friend suggested I go to Ghana Education Trust Fund (GetFund) which, I did, but they kept tossing me till I gave up. I figured out my letter wasn't even read in the first place. I later realized that to get a scholarship from GetFund means you should probably be highly connected to someone in power. I knew nobody, but I knew the Big Man up there in the Heavens.

I thus decided to forget about going to pursue my master's degree outside the country and focused on doing it here in Ghana instead. I started looking for ways to raise my fees so I could pay when I gain admission. The admission list was later released, and my name was part. Hurray. The admission process was delayed, so we had a space of just one week to make all payments and go to school.

Getting a hall was another challenge. I had to apply for it online after admission. The university announced the day the halls would be opened online. Every student was alert behind their computers. I'm so grateful to our department's computer lab technician, Moses. He saved me. Knowing how competitive the situation was, I gave him my student ID number and password to apply for me when the portal was opened. Fortunately, his application went through for me. He managed to get me the most affordable graduate hostel on campus. I was happy. The halls were full in less than 2 minutes after the portal was opened. While many of the students kept complaining, I walked out of the lab with a sunny face.

After doing all the calculations, I realized I could pay only 70 percent of my tuition fee. By some divine direction I went to the lecturer who had supervised my dissertation at the undergraduate level, and had been my boss during national service. Having heard me out, he drove me straight to an Automated Teller Machine and withdrew GHS1,000 for me to pay my hall fees. This philanthropist is Reverend

Dr. Edward Ebo Onumah, the Presiding Elder of Living Word Assemblies of God Church, Ghana.

I further borrowed GHS2,500 from a friend, Anderson, to make full payment of my first year's school fees. I was sorted for the first year to be in school, but had the debt (money borrowed from Anderson) hanging around my neck. With nowhere else to look for help, I mustered courage and went to Prophet Bernard again for help. I pleaded with him that I would need his help this time too, knowing he had already canceled his scholarship scheme because of the ungratefulness of some beneficiaries. This he mentioned during one of his sermons in church. For my request, I did not get an immediate response, but fortunately for me, when my loan repayment time was getting closer, I was in class one day when I received a call from Prophet Bernard to come to his house the following day. I went, and he gave me a cheque of GHS4,460 exactly what

I needed to pay off my loan and purchase the handouts and textbooks.

Later on, I managed to raise money to buy my first laptop. I felt like screaming right there. It was one of the exciting moments in my life as I reflected on all the struggles I had to go through because I did not have a laptop; the only one I had been given by a friend had gotten stolen along with a borrowed one. With this bad experience still on my mind, I guarded the laptop jealously with passion and care. I cleaned it and designed it with some pink stickers.

Aside my studies which I took very seriously, I joined the class group discussions whenever the exams were approaching. The first year came to an end all too soon, and that was how God saw me through.

# Feed the Future Scholar Scholarship

*January 2019*

I remember skipping class for weeks to go for data collection gigs. I did this so I could gather enough money for my second years' tuition. I did not want to go to Prophet Bernard again, and I did not want to borrow. As the first year ended, a friend and a course mate who is now a reliable partner of my charity organization told me she saw some scholarship notice on the department's notice board. She shared a screenshot with me on WhatsApp, and I applied.

Before that, I had gone for an interview for another scholarship I applied for in the middle of the second semester. During that interview, I managed to convince the panelists to grant my application. I was quiet positive about this because of the response I had from the panelist. They showed so much emotion. As at the time of preparing for the interview of the new opening, I was yet to receive any feedback regarding the former. At the interview, God being so good, I found out that the project manager on that scholarship scheme was my principal supervisor, Professor Daniel Bruce Sarpong. The interview went well, but they needed three ladies, and we were four in number. That year, they had to change the scholarship protocol so they could pick all four of us. God be praised!

How relieved I was! Finally, my second year's tuition was fully covered, including my hostel fees and my feeding allowance.

Being a USAID *Feed the Future Scholar* came with many opportunities, including workshops and meetings with allowances. It was indeed an excellent opportunity for me. Thanks to all the project team members, especially Professor Sarpong and Professor Irene Egyir, for their support. This scholarship saved me from much distress. I could sleep without having to think about what to eat the following day or waking up in the middle of the night to shed tears about how I was going to survive the next day. I was able to settle a few bills and save money to buy a few things I needed.

With peace of mind now, I started collecting data for my thesis. This time, my sample size was 300. I looked at how climate change affected Small-Scale Fishers and how these Small-Scale Fishers used the livelihood assets at their disposal to combat these effects from climate change in the coastal Regions of Ghana. After my data collection, I started writing my thesis. It was one of the most challenging parts of my Master of Philosophy (Mphil) studies as my results were giving me difficulties. I got some friends to assist, and finally, I submitted it to the graduate school. Graduation was scheduled for July 2020, but due to the COVID-19 pandemic, it was postponed to November 2020.

# Chapter 13

## THE CORPORATE WORLD

### The way forward after school

*September 2019*

After I submitted my thesis in August 2019, I asked myself, 'what next?' All this while, I had been managing my charity organization alongside. It was very tough—combining running a charity foundation with academics. Running the charity organization came with yearly renewals of the certificate at the Registrar General's Department, renewal of domain hosting, checking up on volunteers, donors, and partners, planning projects, making calls to monitor projects, raising funds, and managing all the social media pages of the organization. I was doing that and still do even as I write this book.

## Housing

My M.Phil. Studies were over, and the hall management asked that we submit the keys and move out. Where next? I had saved some money for rent from my stipends while in school.

Getting a secured place to stay after I left the Home had been a big headache. This was because I could not afford to rent as most landlords' demanded two years rent in advance. I resorted to perching with friends. On a few occasions where I gathered some money, I would pay and stay on campus during my undergraduate studies as that helped me get data collection job offers. I had interactions with some of my orphanage brothers and sisters who stayed and are still staying with friends after they left the Home, and from what they tell me, the stress they go through has never been pleasant. Until late 2019 when I was able to gather some money to rent a place for myself, staying with friends was the norm for me, and the challenges that came with it were unbearable. After almost a year of being at my rented place, I had to look for another place because the cost was too much for me to bear. Accommodation has been one of the major issues care leavers face. This is because getting a secured accommodation is usually expensive. It is considered cheap when care leavers have to share with strangers in the community. Such offers also come with their encumbrances. There is no longer someone to guide such care leavers once they move out of the Home. Institutionalization creates a dependency syndrome which becomes a barrier to novelty sometimes. The transition process into adulthood for care leavers is always abrupt compared to other young people and need to be addressed.

The future is forward inclined, not backward. Most of my orphanage brothers and sisters who left the Home preferred to stay with friends and hustle for secured accommodation than to go back to live with their relatives. The reason is that most don't get the full support needed from these relatives. Most of these relatives had other equally pressing responsibilities; hence an additional mouth to feed seem burdensome. This accounts for the cold attitude most relatives put up towards care leavers. I remember this unpleasant experience of consistently having to go to bed very late- after everyone else in the household had gone to bed, yet having to wake up at 5am to sit outside because I was sleeping in the hall. This was a first hand experience during one vacation when I decided to visit one of my cousins. I know you are wondering why I would go through that stress when I have my parents alive. I did that to secure job offers as going back to live with my mum or dad in the village wouldn't offer me such opportunities, plus the environment at the Home was not that comfortable despite the efforts made by the care givers.

## Becoming Gainfully Employed

A few remarkable people have entered into my life at critical times and helped me mold my thinking pattern. Some changed the entire course of my life. I also look up to these people as mentors. One such mentor is Dr. Charity Osei Amponsah. Dr. Charity, as her name is radiates honesty, warmth, and love. She is dark in complexion and very decent with her dressing. Though married and blessed with three adorable kids, she still has this young and fit look.

She always told me to come to her whenever I faced any challenges, so I sent her a message and told her all the problems I was facing, including my unemployment.

She first congratulated me on finishing school and offered to give me a dinner treat. We settled at Campus Hub one evening. That meeting was another turning point of my life.

Sometimes, all you need is a mentor who has been where you are. We spoke at length, and she promised to notify me of any job opening. She bought me food and drinks. I poured my heart out to her, and she shared a lot with me. She encouraged me not to give up but rather to keep my hopes alive. We parted ways, and that memory we shared that day still lingers with me.

In the third week of August, she sent me a job offer published in the Daily Graphic. It was a Project Officer position with Good Neighbors Ghana-a South Korean based NGO. I quickly applied and received a call the following week to come for an interview. Was that God working on my behalf? I learned all the things I needed to learn. Dr. (Mrs.) Amponsah sent me some interview tips and money for my transportation. She asked me not to go to the interview with public transport but rather go with a private chauffeur driven transport service, so I don't sweat. Indeed, there are many angels here on earth, and I thank God for bringing them my way. I met devils too… but the angels outweighed them.

I went for the interview and realized I was the only lady. We were given a test to write a business proposal for a social enterprise. I had a similar thing for my charity organization, so I used that as a guide and submitted it. We were then called one after the other into the interview room, and I happened to be the last person. I was the smallest and cutest as well. When it got to my turn, it was as if the host of angels went with me. All the questions were about my background and the charity organization I was running. These people did not know they had touched my soft spot. I spoke from my heart and that got them emotional. I became nervous as well at a point in time. The conversation changed to "Do you have a boyfriend?". They pressed my other soft spot. I spoke with enthusiasm, and then finally, I was asked if I had additional questions. Yes, I did. I asked them about their organization and how they were faring in Ghana since they were new here. That got them excited too.

Everything happened so fast that I received a congratulatory message that I had been given the job the following week. I could not believe my ears. I started practicing how I would walk in my heels and how I was going to greet my boss, among other things. I went on a searching spree in my wardrobe to look for some perfect outfit for the workplace. I could count more than six of them. I finally settled on one. I broke the news to Dr. (Mrs.) Amponsah, and she was so excited for me. Thus, I started working in less than a month after completing my master's degree. I had heard many stories about people not getting jobs after school, but my case was different. All praise to God.

I was assigned to a department called the Social Economy Department. We were two in the department—the consultant, Mr. Jang-Hee Im (affectionately called Mr. Im), and

I. Our task was to identify business models that focused on empowering communities. Great things started happening: meetings with stakeholders, bosses, coupled with traveling by air and by road. The feeling was exceptional as I got to meet many people—amazing ones, for that matter. There were people whose names I used to hear and wonder whether I would ever meet them in this life; I found myself sitting right before them. Mr. Im, the consultant, took me as his daughter. He corrected me when I went wrong and always encouraged me. He is a fantastic soul who made me love Koreans more. His kind is unique.

Three months after I started working at Good Neighbors Ghana, he left for the Korean International Cooperation Agency (KOICA) because his contract had ended with Good Neighbors Ghana. Even though he left me, he would still call to find out how I was faring. He is currently serving as the country Director for KOICA in Kenya. I have a lot more experience in NGO management because I had worked with an international one. I'm looking forward to building the Charis Touch Foundation to an international standard.

**Mr. Im and Dzifah during a staff retreat in the Western Region.**

# *Chapter 14*

## OTHER PERSONAL DEVELOPMENT

### The Amazing Woman Award

*March 2020*

My charity works once took me to an orphanage, and the poor state of the infrastructure there made my team and I decide to build a girl's dormitory for them. The orphanage is located in the Oti Region of Ghana. I got my team and other sister NGOs on board to create awareness and raise funds. The kids lived in mud houses, which were not safe for them. At a point, I lost almost all the NGOs I brought together because the money involved was probably beyond them. So, I spoke to my coolest paddy, Ms. Adedolapo Alabi, and she agreed to go all out with me. Sometimes, it isn't about the quantity but the commitment.

I correctly understood that you don't need everyone on your side to succeed. You only need a few right people. Days turned into weeks and weeks into months, and gradually, we got the girls' dormitory completed. It was a fantastic feeling because I never dreamt, we could finish that early. Today, the kids at Blessing Academy Orphanage have a place to lay their heads.

I would say it is this project that earned me the Amazing Woman Award. I did not even know it existed. A friend just asked for my profile and picture. She is the Co-Founder of the Child Crest Foundation. I sent it to her thinking it was one of the usual stuff she was going to use it for; like endorsing sponsorship proposal letters to organizations. She later invited me for a program at Tomreik hotel, and I gladly went. That was where I got the surprise of my life—The International Women Association honored me that day together with my friend as the amazing women for 2020, other women inclusive. The feeling was unique as I sat at the high table with my plague and the shuttering sound of cameras all around me.

**I (Dzifah), displaying the Amazing Woman Award plague at Tomreik hotel in Accra, March 2020**

**Picking Up the Strength in Me.**

There, at the fantastic global women program, one woman had cancer and was undergoing chemotherapy but was still teaching young girls how to make fascinators. Even on the day of the program, she was supposed to start her chemotherapy the next day, and yet, that did not stop her from showing up in connection to a selfless cause she was pursuing. I got shocked that day about the woman's obsession. Indeed, there are beautiful souls all over the world, and I met one that day. Her story has remained with me to date and inspired me to help others, even in my bleakest moments. I devoted myself to reading… reading all kinds of books, from leadership to lifestyle to entrepreneurship to love and marriage to biographies. I will share a couple of those books with you to also read in the subsequent pages. I hope it helps.

While I express my vision and dream for care leavers, orphans and the vulnerable through my interactions, articles, and books,

I hope to get a bigger platform to engage in useful dialogues to help devise great strategies for them. My journey is indeed an account of a life full of happenings that if I were to write them all in this book, there wouldn't be enough space.

This book is not meant to be an entire account of my life. For nearly 15 years, hard work, silence, learning, compassion, and forgiveness, prayers with faith have been the keystone of my life. I have now shared with the world a bit of it. I still have a lot to learn and more notable events and places to discover, and most importantly, I have an amazing future family to raise.

I believe the years ahead will be splendid. I want to be a lecturer/consultant and own chains of businesses aside the NGO I am running. I look back over the years, and I smile. The dots are connecting now. I have come to conclude that there is a reason for everything. I have had numerous painful experiences:

betrayal, hunger, loneliness, and many more, but through it all, I never lost my focus

Having come thus far, I cannot be angry at God or regret experiencing childhood in an orphanage. I consider it to be an open door rather than a revile. You wouldn't have read this lovely story if all went rosy with me (that is, if I had grown up with my parents). You would not have understood the real struggles of care leavers. Like a seed in the soil, I was buried to grow.

# *Chapter 15*

## LETTERS TO STAKEHOLDERS

Meaningful developments for children and youth growing up in care homes can only be made in partnership with care leavers who have experienced the care system. The solution lies in the wisdom of lived experiences of care leavers who know what is at stake towards a significant and lasting change. This epoch's prerequisite is to hear the unheeded voices of care leavers and provide them a plinth to improve on the support system and opportunities available to them, especially bearing in mind that the care system exists for their benefit. Given that, I have put together some useful letters to all stakeholders involved in the welfare of OVCs and care leavers.

**Dear SPONSOR,**

Do not only care about paying for the tuition of a care leaver. Please try as much as possible to get involved in their day to day affairs. They need that a lot too. A little love is all they need, and I know you can give that to them.

Spending quality time with care leavers sparks in them some unique confidence and a sense of being loved. For instance, taking a care leaver, orphan, or a vulnerable child occasionally to a recreational or relaxation centers such as beaches will boost their self-confidence and give them good exposure. Such a demonstration of personal love will also make them open up to you on all the detailed events in their lives.

Also, please never make a promise you cannot keep. I know circumstances do happen which are sometimes beyond one's control, but please try as much as possible to redeem  the little promises you make to these care leavers as they hold unto them dearly. If you promised to help them through school, please don't leave them halfway since they get more depressed in that state with no one to turn to.


## Dear POLICYMAKER,

It is excellent to know all the policies you have in place for OVCs/Care leavers. But I think it would be more appropriate to engage these OVCs/Care leavers in the decision-making process rather than ignore them and bring out policies that may not be favorable to them in the long run. Yes, they may not be of age to make such high-level decisions but paying attention to their voices could help come up with more favorable policies.

Per what I have witnessed, every child at the orphanage I grew up in feared to be adopted on the grounds that if they could not be with their relatives, another  family won't do any better. I remember some of my brothers and sisters at the Home would go into hiding when their prospective adopters came around. In the real world, where half a million children are wards of the state and thousands more will become orphans as their parent(s) die of acquired immune deficiency syndrome, children who cannot be raised by parents need a range of options, with the choice for each to be made based on what is best for him or her

My point is that orphanages may not work for every child. Neither will adoption nor foster care system work for every child. Thus, it is appropriate that the children are taken through the process that best works for them rather than imposing some already made blanket policies on them. It hurts sometimes. Please try and hear these OVCs (Orphan and Vulnerable Children)/care leavers out on what suits them best.

In 2006, the Care Reform Initiative (CRI) and Ghana's Department of Social Welfare (DSW) called for the deinstitutionalization of orphanages and sought to move vulnerable children towards a range of integrated family's community-based care services.

Over a decade after the official launch of the initiative, a myriad of challenges still persists, especially the uncertainty over whether families are prepared to welcome OVCs/care leavers into their homes.

We need to put imagery and politics aside and recognize what liberals and conservatives can agree on: Not every parent can provide for a child, and government must step in when that child is endangered. But just as abuse is not indigenous to one type of child care, so not every child succeeds in a family and not every residential home is a warehouse.

## Deinstitutionalization of residential homes – My take

I am not against the deinstitutionalization of Residential Homes, but I suggest more work needs to be done thoroughly. I think the CRI should be tailored to suit our local context else, we will end up putting rectangular pegs in round holes. Other countries have enforced the foster care system, which doesn't mean it will work here in Ghana. I have witnessed kids running back to the orphanage after they were reintegrated back into the family setting. The maltreatment and the neglect some of them faced was so unbearable for them. They are thus reiterating the point that the foster system may not work for every child. It will be prudent to put each child through a process that works for them as growing up with a family may mean different things to OVCs/ care leavers. Also, I strongly recommend that OVCs/care leavers who will eventually be reintegrated to their families should be helped to stand on their feet and become independent before such actions are taken.

The foster-care program has proved beneficial for many needy or abandoned or mistreated children. However, I feel that most children who are intellectually and emotionally capable of following well planned programs and are capable of taking care of their basic needs would benefit greatly through growing up in large orphanage-type institutions, rather than in foster-care families, a good number of which may themselves be unstable. I believe that these institutions have much to offer, on condition that they are well run administratively and so structured that the children would be supervised by caring adults trained for this vocation. The supervisors should have state certification; such as exists for psychiatric technicians and other health workers in Ghana and in many other countries.

## Dear PASTOR/CHURCH,

Your help for the care leaver should not be tied to the fellow attending your church or perhaps rendering a particular service to you. The care leaver must genuinely decide to join your church. It should never be under compulsion. This applies to any individual offering help to a care leaver. Forcing them to do things out of their interest for you just because you offer them some form of help makes them go through a lot more psychological stress than you can ever think of.

It is recommended that sponsorship should be given freely and not tied to a benefit. For instance, I joined my guardian's church, not because he forced me to. I joined willingly because I wanted to join, and that should be the case.

**Dear RELATIVE,**

It hurts to confirm our belief that you never cared for us in the first place. Every care leaver has the perception that they are not loved by their relations. Please do well to visit them while they are still at the care home and try to support in the little way that you can even after they leave the residential care facilities. Please try to get them involved in your personal lives as well. It means a lot to them. It gives them a sense of belonging.

**Dear CARE LEAVER,**

You have already been through a lot and must learn to be strong for yourself. The world doesn't know a care leaver and a non-care leaver. Grab every opportunity that comes your way and be ready to adapt to the varying phases of life. Go on a personal journey to seek knowledge in books and everywhere that you find it.

Rely solely on God as He is the father to the fatherless. On the roller-coaster of love, dear young care leaver, please be vigilant. Before you give your heart to anyone, I hope you will first give it to yourself. I made the mistake of letting others define me and only loving myself when someone else approved it. I put my self-confidence in their words and actions towards me. I did not realize that I needed to love myself first.

After learning to love yourself first and being ready to start dating, I hope you will look for the right person. Don't just settle for who comes around first. Never fall for anyone's appearance, but rather their personality. The latter and the former are different! Look for someone you can trust and not the one who wants to keep their relationship with you a secret. Look for someone who respects your person, your body, your values, and one you can cherish back. I want you to feel comfortable about yourself and love your body so you can stand proud of who you are every day.

Flee from anyone who shows no enthusiasm about you yet is not ready to part ways with you. Runaway from anyone who makes you disobey God and sin against your own body.

When you get committed to a relationship, I hope you will think twice about saving sex before marriage. I know this isn't the norm these days, but I have seen some pop stars with purity rings. Runaway from anyone who devalues the things of God, and anyone who lies and, when caught, will cover it up with more lies.

It is crucial to me that you get all the right information so you can make better decisions.

# *Chapter 16*

## BEYOND THE ORPHANAGE LIES
## THE REAL STRUGGLE

## How Do Orphans Transition from the
## Various Orphanages into Society?

I believe you have been asking yourself this question. It will interest you to know that there are no laid down procedures guiding how orphans' transition from the orphanages into the community. According to the law at 18 years they need to be outside the institution. This is because the institution is for children and children are defined by age. At 18 years they are adults.

All children deserve a loving family, and the family can appear different depending on the circumstances. Residential institutions are viable options for some children, study says.

But the next question is what next after they leave the four walls of the Care Homes? Do we leave the children to wander around without any substantial support? Do we reintegrate them into their families for reintegrating sake? Most of my siblings at the care home could not see their ambitions fulfilled after reintegrating into the family-based care system. Some had to resort to doing menial jobs to survive because they never got anyone to help them pursue their dreams.

Others had to go through life the hard way to get to the top. Imagine rearing your favorite pet till it outgrows its cage and then; you push it out of the cage without building a new cage for it but rather allowing it to wander around. This scenario can be likened to denying care leavers the necessary support when they leave the orphanage.

According to section 205 of the 1998 Children's Act, every child who clocks 18 years is considered an adult. Given this, once any child in an orphanage turns 18 years, they are asked to leave these care homes to reunite with their families and continue with their lives. Though this is technically accurate, the question I ask myself is the age regardless, are these 'adults' ready to face life outside of the care homes? How have they been prepared to integrate into the community and make a meaningful life?

Inasmuch as the government is encouraging the foster care system, I think there is an equal need for more attention to be given to care leavers so that the investments of good-hearted members of society who supported the care of these children in the care homes will not go wasted. I believe the fear of every child about to transition from a residential home into the real world resonates with the poem below:

*I am seventeen, soon to be eighteen, I'll be thrown out,*

*But the world is so loud. How will I fight?*

*Tell me, is it right?*

*I need an Aftercare home, Same like my shelter home.*

*Am I not the responsibility of the State?*

*Then why am I left alone at this stage?*

*What about the dreams I aspire to achieve?*

*Will I be guided with rehabilitation planning?*

*Education, friends, relationship and my community, Ooppss!*

*Sorry, I'm not even a part of the society.*

*Wake up authority,*

*gift me my identity,*

*Hear my voice screaming for unanswered questions.*

*Understand me, even I have potential, hold my hand, I need a stand.*

*I am seventeen, soon to be eighteen, and eighteen is frightening.*

*By*

*Priyanka Kumari and Suman Kasana*

*(Care Leavers Convention, India)*

Often, because these orphans go through many hands before finally landing at the care homes, many tend to outgrow their class in terms of education. That notwithstanding, in most cases, they are made to complete at least JHS before being asked to leave the care homes. For instance, in the Home I grew up in, the founder always strived to put every child through SHS because he believed that not much could be done with a JHS certificate.

According to Ghana's Child and Family Welfare Policy, the Department of Social Welfare (DSW) is required to keep regular contact with a care leaver for a period between one to six years. This policy, however, doesn't work in all instances. I believe a couple of reasons are responsible for this, the most prominent of them being lack of resources.

Also, given that Ghana has just over 800 social workers for the entire country the prospects of care leavers being supported by aftercare social workers seem unlikely as Dr. Kwabena Frimpong-Manso stated in one of his research paper (paper cited in appendix) on care leaving in Ghana.

Besides, a clearly defined child policy framework is absent. The Care reform was not accompanied by detailed guidelines or procedures and has only been guided by issue-specific plans. There is thus no sector-wide approach to the provision for children under the reform.

Due to these hitches in our system, many care leavers find it very tough and struggle now to put their lives together after they leave the care homes. Many residential institutions are available to provide accommodation (shelter) and food for these children just within the care but has no long term plan to support them when they leave the home.

This is why I wrote this book: to draw people's attention to life beyond the orphanage and how it could be challenging. Most of my siblings at the Home dropped out of school because of a lack of support. Some could not even get the opportunity to go to SHS, let alone the tertiary institution.

Sir William Deane, Australia's Governor-General (1996–2002), passionately voiced that: "the ultimate test of our worth as Nation is how we treat the most vulnerable and disadvantaged of our people." Young people leaving residential institutions are arguably one of the most vulnerable and disadvantaged groups in society. Compared to most young people, they face particular difficulties accessing educational, employment, and housing opportunities.

As a nation, we need to ensure that some of our young people's 'good news stories' believed in the care system is a reality rather than a rarity.

# Chapter 17

## ADDRESSING THE CHALLENGES

### (Recommendations for All Stakeholder)

The social and economic costs linked with the existing failure to provide leaving care and post-care supports to care leavers are noteworthy both for the individuals involved and the broader community. As a care leaver who has survived the various challenging seasons of life in and beyond the orphanage, I firmly believe that the significant challenges that must be addressed by all levels of government for care leavers include:

**1. Sustaining family relations as children and young people need to know their family most:** Care leavers tend to disconnect from their families and even lose affection for them. Such children become cold and bitter with the mindset that their parent(s) and or relatives hated them.

Most families also tend to forget about the very kids they send to the various orphanages. This, in a way, tends to destroy the cordial relationship and bond that should have existed between care leavers and their relatives. For this reason, many care leavers would prefer staying with friends rather than going back to their relatives.

I remember instances where some of these children who were brought to the Home lived there for many years without anyone visiting them. In my case, it took a very long time to pardon my dad as I saw him to be heartless. Although I do check up on him quite often in recent times, that father-daughter connection isn't there. I believe the bond we share now could have been stronger if he regularly visited when I was still at the care home.

To curb these challenges, all the various alternative childcare systems should consider adopting policies that will encourage relatives to visit these children while they are still in the custody of the state or private residential homes. The care home I grew up in, for instance, has two visiting days every month where relatives come around to visit.

In addition to that, relatives or guardians who intend to send children to the orphanages need to be educated on the importance of coming around to visit their wards.

### 2. Providing support to young people transitioning from Care Homes to independent living

There is currently no support system for care leavers. During a discussion on my show, *Let's Talk Orphanage* on Instagram with a social worker, it was further confirmed that there is no vivid support system for care leavers in Ghana.

Although some very few care homes have put in measures to assist care leavers to become stable in life, those structures are not common. As a nation, we should begin to consider putting policies in place to assist these care leavers transition smoothly to become independent citizens in society.

Personally, it took me a very long time to become independent when I left the Home as I had to depend on friends for food, clothes, accommodation, etc. Even as I write this book, I am not fully independent. There are days I depend on friends for survival. Many of my orphanage siblings have to go through much stress as some fell victims to all manner of terrible situations simply because they had to survive. Several of them, too, keep running from one relative to another because of ill-treatment.

Because of the above mentioned, just re-integrating care leavers into their families alone isn't enough. A lot more support needs to be provided for them to stand on their feet in society.

### 3. Improved involvement of OVCs and Care leavers in decision making

As a nation, we need to pay attention to the voices of care leavers and OVCs in making decisions that concern them. Their voice matters in every step of the decision-making process. More often than not, these individuals are omitted and not included in the very decisions that will affect them. For instance, in Ghana, the social welfare department is hitting on children growing with families instead of institutions; they are more interested in the foster care system and have it as a priority. They believe the foster care system is way better than allowing the children to grow in institutions. Nonetheless, they forget that these children were brought to the care homes by (a) relative(s). In the end, most of these children end up thriving in orphanages than with foster parents.

Thus, instead of imposing a particular system that the state feels is the best on the child, it would rather be expedient for these children to be asked what system they will prefer with details of each system spelled out. This, I believe, will go a long way to better shape the little ones for society than when their voices are ignored, but rather have decisions taken and imposed on them.

As I scrolled through the contents of the Ghana Care Reform Initiative, I asked myself whether the concerns of care leavers were sought before such a policy was drafted. Yes, it was drafted for the betterment of these young people but was their opinion sought? No, it wasn't!

## 4. Increased and timely access to support services, such as physical and mental health and education

Almost every care leaver has experienced a mental health problem one way or the other. For instance, growing up in an orphanage while both of my parents were alive made me think of myself very less sometimes. Although the thought of suicide never came to mind, I battled with an inferiority complex as I felt that probably, I wasn't loved or cherished. This is common with every care leaver.

As these young ones exit the residential homes, it will be prudent to put in place counseling sessions to orient their mindset and understand the new environment they are stepping into. Currently, I am yet to know of the existence of any such structures in Ghana. This tends to badly affect their growth process as they are left to face the strange and unfamiliar societal conditions without prior preparations.

With my little crop science background, I know that before seedlings are transplanted to the main field, they are made to undergo some processes while in the nursery, so they don't get shocked by the new environment, they will soon find themselves in. Before transplanting, they are kept in the shade (which keeps reducing) before being transplanted into the field. This way, they can adjust quickly and efficiently to their new environment. Unfortunately, such structures do not exist for care leavers.

## 5. Technical and Vocational skills set empowerment.

As a nation, I believe that instituting a system where a free technical and vocational training program is put in place for all care leavers will go a long way to equip them with relevant skills that would enable them sustain themselves as they get ready to face the world on their own to make a living.

Not every care leaver would love to go to the tertiary institution. Others would prefer to acquire a technical or vocational skill instead. Back at the Home I grew up in, Citi Fm (one of the famous radio stations in Ghana), together with their partners, built a vocational/technical facility to help the students acquire some skill in carpentry, hairdressing, soap making, tie and dye making, sewing, etc. But the facility lacked instructors and the needed equipment to train the students.

Hence, there is the need for State and private-owned organizations and even individuals to take it upon themselves to adopt an orphanage and help provide some of the necessary materials needed for training these orphans and vulnerable children to acquire a skill. That way, after they leave the Home, they can establish their own businesses to cater for themselves.

Additionally, individual local vocational businesses such as carpentry, hairdressing, etc.

can take it up to provide free slots yearly for at least one orphan, care leaver or vulnerable child to serve as an apprentice in their shops to learn the skill.

I have a friend for instance who teaches orphans beads making and sewing. These are some significant steps we can all take to help such care leavers.

Back in the care home where I grew up, a company that was into curtains production (Eyaqueen) always gave free slots to some of the care leavers to learn the trade, and I can say at least two of them have set up their own curtain businesses. We need more of these companies to assist.

Furthermore, for those who desire to further their education beyond JHS, we need to consider providing both free admission and scholarship slots in the various SHS and tertiary institutions for OVCs who have qualified into any of such institutions. This is to facilitate uninterrupted education or, in most scenarios, prevent dropping out of school and ultimately ending up with unfulfilled dreams and aspirations. These, I believe, can play a significant role in meeting the needs of many of tomorrow's children.

Having being armed with the revelations in this book, please pray for more individuals and institutions to support care leavers. You can be one of such individuals. Your organization can also be one of such organizations.

## Recommended Formal Education Support Systems

A research done by UNICEF in 2010 estimates that there are over one million orphans in Ghana, with about 4,500 children in orphanages. As of 2016, there were about 115 residential childcare centers in Ghana. There are also forty-six (46) Colleges of Education (e.g., Teacher and Nurses Training Institutions, etc.) as well as Ten (10) universities in Ghana, according to the National Accreditation Board's 2016 summary. According to a 2016 Ghana Education Service data cited on *citifmonline,* there are about eight hundred and seventy-two (872) SHSs in Ghana.

Now check this breakdown out:

Granted that a slot is reserved for a care leaver in each of the SHSs would mean that 872 care leavers will be enrolled in SHS's every year. Increase the number of slots to two, and we will have times two of the number, which is incredibly impressive.

**NB**: By a slot, I am explicitly referring to provisions for both admissions and scholarships.

| Number of SHS in Ghana | One free slot for JHS graduate care leaver | Two free slots for JHS graduate care leavers |
|---|---|---|
| 872 | 872 care leavers will be enrolled in SHS every year | 1,744 care leavers will be enrolled in SHS every year |

Thank God there is now a free SHS policy in Ghana. Hence all stakeholders can support a care leaver in SHS by providing for them their basic needs including safe housing etc.

## How about the Tertiary Institutions?

As stated earlier above, there are about 46 Colleges of Education and over ten universities in Ghana. If each tertiary institution provided at least three slots every year for care leavers, the results will be incredibly significant. That would mean 136 care leavers going to the various Colleges of Education and 10 care leavers to the tertiary institutions every year. Also, these tertiary institutions could waive off a part of the fees. Say, 50 to 70 percent waiver. That way, it would be easier to get sponsors quickly for these care leavers. For instance, a full scholarship in Ghana's public university ranges from 4500 to 5500 Ghana Cedis yearly (the University of Ghana, 2020). This means a waiver of 50 or 70 percent is a big deal for potential sponsors.

## How about Churches and other Religious Institutions?

In an article cited on www.dw.com, there were more than ten thousand (10,000) churches in Ghana as of 2014. This figure is likely to have significantly increased by now (2020). But for the sake of simplicity, let's stick to the 2014 statistics. Now, imagine each of these churches sponsored one or two care leaver (s) to pursue higher education (both at the high school and tertiary level); I hope you know what that means. See the computation below:

| Number of churches in Ghana | One free slot for JHS and SHS graduate care leaver | Two free slots for JHS and SHS graduate care leavers |
|---|---|---|
| 10,000 | 10,000 care leavers will be enrolled in SHS and Tertiary Institutions every year | 20,000 care leavers will be enrolled in SHS and tertiary institutions every year |

The Family Based Care Alliance has launched an initiative where all churches are called upon to support orphans in their communities and churches. I suggest churches embark on a policy called *one OVC one church*. Also, churches should partner with orphanages by serving as foster parents to these orphanages. The seasonal donation of food and drinks to orphanages by churches should rather be made monthly. In between the seasonal donations, have you wondered what these young ones feed on? Now, imagine that the mosques and other religious institutions replicate this strategy, we would be impacting the lives of many of these vulnerable children.

## How about Individuals?

I was sponsored by one Man-Prophet Bernard El Bernard Nelson Eshun (The General Overseer of Spiritlife Revival Ministries), to pursue my undergraduate and a part of my postgraduate studies. Ghana's population currently stands at thirty-one million, seventy-one thousand, three hundred and twenty-two (*31,071,332*) as of Friday, July 3, 2020, based on Worldometer elaboration of the latest United Nations data. If at least 0.1 percent of the population, thirty-one thousand and seventy-one (31,071) decide to offer a scholarship to one orphan or vulnerable child to go to school and pursue their dream career, we will all attest to the fact that a lot more lives will be touched.

Kindly repeat this computation for your country and see what significant impact we all will leave in the lives of care leavers. If considered and implemented, these few practical recommendations will go a long way to make the lives of OVCs and care leavers better and facilitate their smooth transition from the orphanages into the society as they will be adequately equipped to face life on their own.

Also, future directions should be built on this progress and should consider how government and service organizations can achieve the following:

1. Enhanced education opportunities for young people in and out of Homecare.

2. Reinforced transition supports from primary to secondary school for young people at the risk of dropping out.

3. Strengthened co-operative planning for young people as they move to independence.

4. Underwired family re-connection initiatives that suit the ranges of needs of young people and families.

5. Strengthened mentoring programs, especially about vocation, pre-employment, and employment support roles.

6. A more excellent range of housing and housing models that consider young people's needs, especially about affordability.

## Some Institutions that give support to needy children in Ghana

Few institutions give support to needy but brilliant students, and it is appropriate that we have more of such organizations focusing on only care leavers from the residential institutions across the country.

~MTN Ghana Scholarship

~Ghana Scholarship Fund

~Citi Opportunity Project on Education (COPE)

~Ghana Education Trust Fund

~Vodafone Ghana Foundation Scholarship Scheme

When I was about to start my master's program, a scholarship from Cocoa Board came and the conditions attached was unbelievable. To be considered as a beneficiary of the scholarship, one had to pay thousands of Ghana Cedis. As soon as I realized that, I had to let go of the offer. I kept asking myself how and when we got to this stage. What happens to that care leaver who managed to get some good grades and doesn't even have what it takes to pay for protocol fees or what have you?

Later on, in the middle of the semester, all my friends who got the money to pay the protocol fees got the scholarship. I only shrugged, "All is well." Some of my mates did not need the scholarship but got it anyway. What a world!

I suggest many modifications be made to suit those needy students'/care leavers in this category. Maybe a national network for the education of care leavers should be established in every country to support them pursue higher education.

## Food for thought

Journeying out into the world on your own for the first time is thrilling and overwhelming for all of us. The chance to carve your own path and the newfound independence is a vast draw. Then again, learning to be economical to keep on top of the bills, remembering to put a wash on in time so that you have clean clothes for work on Monday morning, and managing to keep the fridge stocked, let alone keeping yourself healthy; it's a huge learning curve for any young person. It's even more difficult for those deprived of supportive families to fall back on, or for those who can't stay at home for other reasons.

Those who have grown up, or spent time, in care don't always have the luxury of a family home to return to if something goes wrong, or a parent to phone when they aren't sure how to fix a problem. Nonetheless, you and me can change the narrative.

# Chapter 18

## THE CHARIS TOUCH FOUNDATION

### About Charis Touch Foundation (CTF)

All evidence points in the same direction: the best way to be happy in life is to be a little less concerned with oneself and be a bit more caring about others. I established this Foundation to give back to society. Starting this NGO led to my total transformation. I love to help OVCs and care leavers, and sometimes, I am tempted to believe this is why I was brought into this world and why I had to go through all that I experienced.

My aim for writing this book is to raise my voice for the other millions of care leavers across the globe who face real difficulty. My mission is to mobilize resources for addressing the challenges facing OVCs and care leavers to enable them realize their full potentials by promoting programs on education, health care, recreational skills, shelter, social security, and moral support.

I hope that all of you will join this cause to make living worthwhile for these young heroes and heroines. Yes! I call them such because they are conquerors and warriors and even much more. They are better than that.

Find out more at www.charistouchworld.org.

# Chapter 19

## WHAT LIFE TAUGHT ME

### To My Avid Readers

I have had a lot of failed ambitions and plans. I have experienced many disappointments from friends and loved ones. But that never stopped me from dreaming. Yes! To some, I did not have the looks, but that did not discourage me. I was recently advising a young girl who is now my mentee to study hard and ignore the fact that people do not want to associate with her. I advised her to learn so hard, and it would pave a way for her very soon.

You are a decision away from leaving any bad life behind and embracing a whole new life. You are a decision away from becoming that person you want to become. Do not stay at the same place, same position, same thoughts, and with the same attitude.

Whatever you allow will keep happening in your life. Take that bold decision today and forget about how that decision will make others feel about you. Once that decision gives you inner peace, fulfillment, and connects you to your Maker, go ahead and make it.

Remember, you are always a decision away. Please don't wait until it is too late.

I believe in victims' stories because I know firsthand about the shame and stigma that comes with raising your hand and saying, "this happened to me."

Did you ever suffer any abuse while growing up? It could be emotional, sexual, physical, verbal, etc. If yes, how are you coping with it? Are you healed? If you have healed from your wounds, congratulations. If not, it is never too late to do so now.

It is needful to work on your past and heal from all the pains you suffered from childhood. This is because realizing and doing what it takes to heal from your wounds will make you enjoy adulthood. You can confide in a counselor, a trusted friend, or pray to God for strength. Do not worry about the hands that will point at you when you are going through your healing process. Whatever bad past (scars) you refuse to deal with now will come back and haunt you.

It takes some level of boldness to fix your past wounds, but doing it makes you free. Release forgiveness to anyone who caused you pain apologize to those you wronged and embrace that new self. No more hesitations; deal with those wounds.

**Never Give Up in Life**

Are you on the verge of giving up? Or, have you given up already? There are times you try to hold on to certain things with all you have, and suddenly, that thing fails. You may have labored with all you had to build that business, but it came crashing down.

All along, there seem to be many trials (rejections, failures, heartbreaks, disappointments, etc.) with no end, but God's word declares the truth.

You may be on a journey that seems so long. The burden of you walking alone on that road may sometimes be unbearable. But can I tell you something? There will be a day, and that day is so close when everything will fall in place for you—a day when the burdens of your present circumstance will be no more. Remember, there are a reason and time for everything under the sun. Problems come with their goals and purpose. Every hatred has a purpose. Every friend has a purpose. Every rejection has a purpose. Don't be too hard on yourself, forgive yourself, move on, and allow time to heal you of every wound.

One morning on my way to work, I had to wait for a friend at a particular bus stop, so we join the same bus to the office. While standing and waiting, I saw a mad man deeply asleep in front of a shop. Within a space of seconds, a man from nowhere threw a massive box in the direction where the mad man was sleeping. Thinking he will be agitated to wake up, this mad man turned and slept again—this time in a better position. I was wowed. I learned never to give up on that day.

## Cry No More

The longer the wait, the bigger the gift. The person you are becoming will cost you many things but choose YOU over them all. Stop struggling to meet public expectations, start fighting for your vision, dreams, ideas, and destiny. While fighting for all of these things, remember there will be a day in your life where you will experience no more tears, no more pain, and no more fears, but until that day comes, hold unto to God always.

There has never been a step Where you've walked out all alone. He is Emmanuel (God with us). Nothing remains the same in this world. Whatever situation you are going through may not end when you want it to stop, but trust me, it will come to an end. Nothing remains permanent under the sun except the word of God.

Knowing this truth will save you from much stress. You may have experienced some lousy situation a decade ago, but you only laugh about it now when you remember, right? That is the same way the situation you are facing today will end, and you will laugh about it in the next decade when you remember it. Oh, yes, it inevitably will end.

Some of the experiences may leave apparent wounds, but with time, they will all heal. Beating yourself up would not help. Relax and take a deep breath when you encounter bad situations, knowing that they will all come to an end.

After all, we live in a temporal world, and so is every situation or challenge.

We often tend to worsen our misfortunes by forgetting there are valuable lessons we can learn from them. Instead of getting upset and sad, there is a better way to approach these issues to bring so much joy and peace and refreshment to your soul.

## Everything Has a Purpose

Whatever pain you are going through today, always remember that there is a purpose in that pain. Many people are locked up in the past so much that they cannot move on in life. Remember that the Holy book (Bible) says there is no temptation that has overtaken you that is not common to man. This is to let you know that others have survived the same thing no matter what you are going through. Why kill yourself? Why are you throwing a pity party for yourself because of your past?

Why don't you see things from a different perspective? Always remember that we live in a temporal world, and so are your problems. That problem, too, will pass. Look up to your Maker for divine help to overcome whatever pain you are battling with. Growing up in an orphanage, I have every reason to be angry and blame God and the people around me for all the painful experiences. But I learned over the years and discovered that there is a purpose in whatever pain you suffer here on earth. That inspired me to start an NGO that supports the less privileged in society. Inside that pain is hidden your weapon of success.

After you have survived the pain:

1. Let it go.

2. Embrace the lessons learned and share

to bless other people.

3. Remember that as far as you are human and continue to breathe, pain is inevitable, but how you handle, it matters a lot.

## Everyone Slips and Falls

Sometimes you sit down somewhere — maybe in your room, at the office, or in front of your TV, and out of nowhere, a thought pops up in your mind: "Why was I taken for granted?" Or you realize you have messed up big time, and you can't just help but blame yourself all over again. Can I tell you something? Stop being hard on yourself. Learn to forgive and let go. Remember that everyone slips and falls.

## Learn to Love Yourself

There are a few more things that you need to learn about loving and accepting yourself. Be kind to yourself. Challenges can sometimes hit a raw nerve within you, but you need to take it to step by step and nurture yourself in the process. Remember, you cannot change other people, the past, or circumstances beyond your control.

Life is amazing. You hit a few road bumps along the way, but eventually, the road gets smooth again. Learning to accept that falling is part of any process will allow you to smile and jump back up again.

Appreciating the good you do all the time you try to help others will allow you to smile and realize that you are already playing your part. No one thought your life could be this hard. Families, relationships, careers, money, and all the other stuff can seem so confusing.

Nobody told you how to avoid getting hurt in life's battles. You can't stop bullets like the killers in movies, yet people unintentionally create holes in your plans, dreams, and heart every day. But you are not alone. Everyone is struggling with something in their life, publicly or privately. Yet, society makes it look like it's unacceptable to talk about it.

So, whenever you attack yourself for not standing up to life's battles, repeat this: "No situation is permanent." Stop beating yourself over everything you think, say, or do. Stop criticizing yourself endlessly for all your so-called weaknesses or shortcomings. Instead, feel good about yourself. Feel great about yourself. Give yourself a break… Look in the mirror and smile at the person smiling back at you because that person is lovely and deserves your love.

## Keep searching till you find

Believe it or not, everyone under the sun is on a journey in search of something valuable. While others are in pursuit of true happiness, others are searching for true love, among others. While others are searching for great jobs, others are searching for ways to make money. You will realize that everyone's search differs from the other. This is why you don't necessarily have to follow the crowd because everyone is on a different journey, searching for that satisfying item.

On this journey, others find what they are searching for very early while others find theirs quite late. Whichever category you belong to, remember that you will lay hold of that particular thing you are searching for if you don't give up. You only need to be focused and identify what you want, and then you can search for it. Otherwise, you will embark on a fruitless search.

Sometimes, the very things we are searching for may be closer than we think, but our eyes may refuse to see them. So always try to look around and within you while exploring. The very things you are searching for may be right inside or near you. Do not be tempted to give up on your search because others got what they were looking for quickly. Keep searching until you lay hold of that thing you have so desired to have.

## Manage your Emotions

Growing up, I always thought the friends and loved ones I grew up with will always be with us. Little did I know it was a terrible mistake on my part to think that way. We can all attest that the people we grew up with will not be the people we will have around all the time. We lose some of these loved ones along the way via several means thinkable, and then we become emotionally unstable. Some of these loved ones leave indelible marks in our hearts. Some friends you make may end up traveling and may never come back; others may get involved in so many other things. These create or bring some form of disconnections, and all these losses and disruptions bring so much emotional instability since we tend to love these people and will always wish they are around us all the time, but suddenly we look around are nowhere to be found. I have suffered a series of emotional turbulence, and I know you may have experienced the same due to the disconnection of loved ones and friends by death, traveling overseas, etc.

To be on the safer side, you should build your emotions such that you get to a level where your feelings no longer face turbulence, and that is what I call emotional independence. Attaining this level of maturity with your emotions will make you healthy and happy all the time. Always understand that no friendship is permanent because we are in a temporal world. Learn to be independent when it comes to matters of emotions. This is because even your shadow leaves you when it gets dark.

A life of emotional independence is one wherein your mood, self-esteem, self-worth, and happiness are your products. Your feelings are independent of theirs. Others don't "make" you sad or happy. You choose your emotional responses to life's circumstances.

This is not to say you wouldn't need others' affection and love. We all need friendship, care, and respect and always wished that our loved ones will be with us forever but then try to be emotionally independent to save you from the stress in situations where things go in opposite directions.

## Keep Working on Yourself

There are times you may have fallen, and you may have been helpless, perplexed, or worse off. Yet, even though you are hurting, you must continue moving. Everyone you meet in life has a role to play in your life; some will utilize and mishandle you; others will cherish and bring out the best in you. Yet, you have to aspire more, keeping in mind the ultimate aim to distinguish whatever role each person needs to play in your life.

A squandered time can never be recuperated, so quit supporting some companionships that you know ultimately will lead nowhere.

Quit crying over that separation or lost occupation. Yes, it hurts, but you need to forge ahead. Remember that regardless of how much people mean to you, it doesn't mean they will esteem you the same way. Keep your head up, because if it's down, you won't have the capacity to see the endowments. Try not to surrender due to one terrible section in your life.

Figure out how to relinquish any individual who has insulted or disillusioned you. Dear one, close that section of your life and never re-read it. Don't try to fix what got broken in your past. Leave the past and move on.

## Overcome Your Fears

A little bit of fear is healthy. But you might find yourself fearful of things that aren't dreadful, like starting a business, stepping out of your comfort zone, starting that friendship, talking about how you feel, etc. The issue of facing your fears is something that everyone deals with. This is because everyone is afraid of something- and that is the truth. That neighbor down the street, your mentor, that celebrity… every Tom, Dick, and Harry.

The big difference is that some people chose to live their lives in fear and be held back, leading to a life full of regret, anger, and frustration, while others prefer to face them, leading to a victorious life. Fear can range from the overpowering desire to look away or stop in your tracks to running from the life you've always desired to have.

Fear and anxiety are like abductors that hold you imprisoned, holding you back from the full, free life you could be living. The dominion of fear on your life will typically get worse over time if left unchecked. There are times when you are faced with the fear of rejection, the fear of failure, and the fear of having to start something new.

Always know that it is human nature to avoid emotions that scare us. Who wants to walk straight into what promises to be a painful experience? You may have been hiding from potential challenges that can lead to growth and joy. But the truth is you can't protect yourself forever from fear. It's going to strike despite your best efforts to suppress it. And it will likely hit at a time when you most needed emotional calmness. So, dare to face your fears by conquering them daily. It is time to deal with all the "what ifs" of life and go all out. Make that phone call today...You may never know the outcome. Fill that application form again...the result might be different this time around. Try to list your fears one after the other and watch yourself overcome them all.

## Be good to all

Most people will not be in our boat, but that they try to understand how we feel means the world. Those who ask you how you're doing and really want to know the answer. Bask in their warmth and treasure this gift of human connection. And then pass that along. We can love and support others in their pain by remembering the darkness we also have faced. Let's walk beside them and give of ourselves. Others' suffering can be different, but let's listen with an open heart, sitting together with them in their darkness stage, holding their hand, not saying a word. That is godly love.

*"It is not what happens to you that determines how far you will go in life: it is how you handle what happens to you".*          *~ZIG ZIGLAR*

# APPENDIX

## OTHER RESOURCES CITED

- Frimpong-Manso, K. (2014). *Child welfare in Ghana: The past, present and future*. Journal of Educational and Social Research, 4(6), 411.

- BERGIN & GARVEY: *The Hebrew National Orphan Home: Memories of Orphanage Life*

- https://today.duke.edu/2014/08/whettenorphans

- https://globalhealth.duke.edu/news/study-finds-orphanages-are-viable-options-some-children

- https://www.washingtonexaminer.com/weekly-standard/the-success-story-of-orphanages

- http://citifmonline.com/2017/09/breakdown-of-the-number-of-schools-in-ghana-infographic/

- http://www.nab.gov.gh/news1/414-accredited-published-tertiary-institutions-as-at-august-2016-summary. Retrieved 2020-05-16 as cited on wikiedia.org

- https://www.dw.com/en/too-many-churches-in-ghana/a 19140778#:~:text=In%202014%20 there%20were%20more,groups%20 claiming%20allegiance%20to%20 Christianity.

- https://www.worldometers.info/world-population/ghana-population/

- file:///C:/Users/Felix%20Larnor/ Downloads/Leaving_care_and_ Homelessness_special_is.pdf

- file:///C:/Users/Felix%20 Larnor/Dropbox/My%20 PC%20(LAPTOP-3SENHVJ1)/ Downloads/06120HEstaff%20(1).pdf

# *Photo Gallery*

Dzifah's first laptop, 2018

Dzifah with a hoe during the groundbreaking session for the construction of the girls' dormitory at Blessing Academy Orphanage-Abotoase

BASCO, The Home Dzifah grew up in.

Dzifah (extreme right) and her SHS classmates in 2010

First outreach of CTF at Dzifah's alma mater -BASCO

Prophet Bernard El Bernard Nelson Eshun, the man who sponsored Dzifah's university education fully at the undergraduate level and partly at the graduate level.

Prophet Vincent Bannerman, Dzifah's Pastor

Join the conversation on Instagram and #letstalkorphanage

# SOCIAL MEDIA PAGES

Let's connect on

- ✓ LinkedIn: https://www.linkedin. com/in/deborah-tamakloe- dzifah-970893125/

- ✓ Facebook: https://www.facebook. com/dzifahtamakloeGH

- ✓ Instagram: https://www.instagram. com/dzifahtamakloe/

- ✓ Kindly visit www.charistouchworld.org for details of what my team and I do

NB: Proceeds from this book goes into advancing the cause of care leavers, orphans and vulnerable children.

For bulk purchases, contact the author:

Deborah Dzifah Tamakloe

+233 (0) 242 125 415

tamakloe.deborah@yahoo.com

# OTHER BOOKS BY THE SAME AUTHOR

1. *Forest In The Wilderness (inside life of a Ghanaian orphanage)*
2. *Great Minds, Great Ideas*

# 21 BOOKS THAT CHANGED MY LIFE!

- *Who Will Cry When You Die?* - Robin Sharma
- *Don't Sweat The Small Stuff* - Richard Carlson
- *The Monk Who Sold His Ferari* - Robin Sharma
- *Who Moved My Cheese?* - Spencer Johnson
- *Thrive* - Ariana Huffington
- *You're A Badass* - Jen Sincero
- *No More Sheet* - Juanita Bynum
- *At Home With Madam Chic* - Jennifer L. Scott
- *Men Are From Mars, Women Are From Venus* - John Gray
- *Love And Respect* - Emerson Eggrichs
- *Sacred Marriage* - Gary Thomas
- *Oliver Twist* - Charles Dickens
- *The Automatic Millionaire* - David Bach
- *Purity And Passion* - Wendy Watson Nelson
- *Secrets Girls Keep* - John Ellsworth
- *The Power Of Now* - Eckart Tolle

- *The Sacred Search* - Gary Thomas
- *Brandraising* - Sarah Durham
- *Outliers* - Malcoim Gladwell
- *The Last Black Unicorn* - Tiffany Haddish
- *Man's Search For Meaning* - Viktor Frankl

All these books are available on https://www.pdfdrive.com

# ABOUT THE AUTHOR

## <u>Meet Deborah Dzifah Tamakloe</u>

Deborah Dzifah Tamakloe grew up in the Baptist School Complex and Orphanage in the Eastern Region of Ghana. As a child from a broken home, Deborah has a remarkable life journey that presents the possibility of rising from utter despair to hope. Facing these obstacles in her own life instilled in her a passionate drive to fight for those who are in the situation she used to be.

Having been moved beyond tears by the stories of these children she grew up with, she promised to give them the voice they did not have.

Deborah is a trained Agricultural Economist and the Charis Touch Foundation founder, an NGO that provides support for orphans and vulnerable children.

Spearing through life's challenges, she has risen to become an author and a speaker.

In Ghana, she was honored with the 2020 Amazing Woman award for her humanitarian work.

Deborah craves to reach out to the world, incredibly the less privileged, with God's infinite love. As a young lady who has been equipped with competence and resilience, Deborah's desire to make the world a better place continues to grow along with her understanding of various social issues.

When Deborah is not writing, she spends most of her time reading, visiting care homes, and listening to her favorite Hillsong worship songs. She is also an Ashoka changemaker, an African Changemaker Alumni, a Kectil Fellow, and a Mentor. She currently serves as Programs Assistant at Good Neighbors Ghana-a South Korean NGO.

Deborah presently resides in Ghana and shares her passion with the world at www. charistouchworld.org.

# REFLECTIONS

Printed in Great Britain
by Amazon